ALBERTO SALAZAR'S GUIDE TO RUNNING

ALBERTO SALAZAR'S

GUIDE TO

RUNNING

A CHAMPION'S REVOLUTIONARY

PROGRAM TO REVITALIZE YOUR FITNESS

ALBERTO SALAZAR
with RICHARD A. LOVETT

RAGGED MOUNTAIN PRESS / McGRAW-HILL

Camden, Maine • New York • Chicago • San Francisco • Lisbon • London • Madrid • Mexico City •
Milan • New Delhi • San Juan • Seoul • Singapore • Sydney • Toronto

Ragged Mountain Press
A Division of The McGraw-Hill Companies

10 9 8 7 6 5 4 3 2 1

Library of Congress Cataloging-in-Publication Data
Salazar, Alberto, 1958–
    Alberto Salazar's guide to running : a champion's revolutionary program to revitalize your fitness / Alberto Salazar with Richard A. Lovett.
        p.   cm.
    Includes index.
    ISBN 0-07-137027-7
        1. Running. 2. Physical fitness. I. Title: Guide to running. II. Lovett, Richard A. III. Title.

GV1061.S22 2001
613.7´172—dc21   00-053324

Questions regarding the content of this book should be addressed to
Ragged Mountain Press
P.O. Box 220
Camden, ME 04843
www.raggedmountainpress.com

Questions regarding the ordering of this book should be addressed to
The McGraw-Hill Companies
Customer Service Department
P.O. Box 547
Blacklick, OH 43004
Retail customers: 1-800-262-4729
Bookstores: 1-800-722-4726

This book is printed on 55-lb Sebago by R. R. Donnelley & Sons, Crawfordsville, IN
Design by Dede Cummings Design
Production by Dede Cummings, Carolyn Kasper, and Dan Kirchoff
Edited by Tom McCarthy and Shana Harrington
Photography by Steve Dipaolo except where otherwise noted
Illustrations by Nancy Benner

CONTENTS

To Don Benedetti, Bill Squires, and Bill Dellinger

ACKNOWLEDGMENTS

PEOPLE LOVE TO SPEAK of the loneliness of the long-distance runner, but nobody truly runs alone. Three coaches were instrumental in my development as a runner. They always did what was best for my long-term success, never pushing merely for short-term accomplishments that would have been more their benefit than mine. For their dedication and shared wisdom, my gratitude goes to my high school coaches—Don Benedetti and Bill Squires—and to my college coach, Bill Dellinger. I'd also like to thank Nike for all the support over the years, not only in sponsoring me financially, but for moral support as well.

For technical assistance in the many areas of writing this book, thanks are due to many people, notably Dr. Kelly Scott for helping maximize medical accuracy, Alistair McColl and Robin Roberts for input on technical aspects of running apparel, Wyatt Brown for advice on orthotics, and OHC in Portland for technical assistance with drawings. I also thank the many sports and human-performance researchers whose careers provided information that not only helped me run better, but which infuses much of this book as well. Many long-time runners shared stories and fielded questions that have wound up being part of this book in one way or another.

I am indebted to Rick Lovett for much of the background research for chapter 8. As a freelance news reporter with a decade-long interest in food science, medicine, and biochemistry, he has attended dozens of scientific conferences and read numerous journal articles about diet, nutrition, and other food-related topics. This book draws heavily on the nearly 1,000 articles he's written on these subjects, as well as the latest reports coming in over his fax even as we were completing the manuscript.

ALBERTO SALAZAR'S GUIDE TO RUNNING

INTRODUCTION

W E LIVE IN AN ERA that has been called the "second running boom." The original boom began in the 1970s when Dr. Kenneth Cooper published his groundbreaking book *Aerobics*, the first major report on the benefits of vigorous exercise. Cooper brought the word *aerobics* into the mainstream and did more than anyone or anything else to spawn the jogging boom of the 1970s, as millions of Americans hit the pavement to chalk up their weekly rations of "aerobics points." Americans have been runners ever since.

Cooper's advice was to rack up 30 of these points a week—roughly the equivalent of running 8 to 10 miles a week. But popular culture has always believed that "if some is good, more must be better." By the 1980s, Americans were hitting the marathon courses in record numbers, producing intense competition just to get into some of the major races.

This focus on running was fueled in part by Frank Shorter's 1972 gold medal and 1976 silver medal in the Olympic marathon. But it was also fueled by highly publicized claims that anyone who ever got into sufficient shape to run a marathon would be forever immune to heart attack—a claim that history has proven simply not to be true. Now we know that you achieve most of the benefit of daily exercise simply by running 15 miles a week—and that there is almost no health advantage to exceeding 5 miles a day.

We also know that while running greatly reduces cardiac risk, no amount of exercise eliminates it completely. People may choose to run longer distances for the challenge or because they enjoy the competition, but if we're honest, even those of us who love long-distance running must admit we don't do it for our health. You can run 2 miles a day with relatively little chance of injury, but once you exceed 5 miles a day, you're at risk of spending more and more time on injured reserve. Furthermore, successful long-distance runners sacrifice upper body strength to keep their weight low (so they can run faster), and they obsess about staying thin.

If your goal is to run as fast as you can, all of this focus on long-distance running is useful. If your goal is to be buff and physically fit, however, you're better off to run less and add a complementary sport, such as bicycling, cross-country skiing, rowing, weight training, or hiking.

> **You don't get much more benefit from training yourself to run 6-minute miles than you do if your top, comfortable pace is 10 minutes or even 12 minutes a mile.**

This is what the new running boom is all about. People are again flocking to the sport, but they're using running as part of an overall health and fitness plan rather than as an end in itself. In the process, they're discovering not only that running is an excellent way to pack a nice dose of exercise into 20 minutes, but that you don't have to be a fanatic for it to become a lot of fun. Rather than crowding the marathons, these people are more likely to be drawn to 3- or 5-mile celebrations of health called "fun runs." These low-key races may not even have a clock. Not only is there little added health benefit to running longer distances, but you don't get much more benefit from training yourself to run 6-minute miles than you do if your top, comfortable pace is 10 minutes or even 12 minutes a mile. The important thing is simply to get your body out and moving—with your heart rate moderately elevated—away from those twin banes of modern health, the refrigerator and the remote-control television.

Many running books don't reflect this reality. They're aimed at racers: teaching how to train for a marathon in six months (or a year), how to shave a few minutes off a 10-kilometer time, or how to maximize speed or distance training. There's nothing wrong with performance-motivated running, but this book is different. Its purpose is to teach you how to integrate running into a healthy lifestyle that you should be able to maintain for decades to come.

Market surveys by shoe companies have indicated that this integration is indeed what most new runners are seeking. In the 1980s, typical first-time shoe buyers were people who'd seen the New York City Marathon on television and were targeting on running their own marathons—often setting the goal before they'd even laced up their shoes for their first tentative jogs. Today's beginning runners, however, are more likely to have no intention of running even a short road race, let alone a marathon. Their goals are more modest—and more sustainable. These people are turning to running as part of an overall fitness program designed to maintain health and alleviate job stress, not to train for specific competitive goals.

If this describes you, this is your book. It will also teach you how to race, if you want, but that's secondary to developing yourself into a runner.

In keeping with these goals, this book advocates a very conservative start-up program, designed to take you from nonathlete to running about 15 miles a week over the course of your first year. It's possible to advance more quickly—and if you're already well-conditioned from another sport, you might find it easy to do so—but the goal is to make sure the transition from nonrunner to runner occurs slowly and gradually. Most people run too far, too quickly, too soon. That's a prescription for giving up in the first few months or—if you tough it out—for always being tired and achy. A better method is to think in the long term, while finding enough enjoyment at each stage of your running career that the prospect of 20, 30, 40, or 50 more years is something to be anticipated with pleasure, not as the equivalent of a prison sentence or an unpleasant medical procedure.

To reinforce the idea that your integration into running is best done as a gradual transition, this book is divided into two parts, modeled on a sequence of academic courses. Each part even has a suggested midterm and final "exam."

The first part, Running 101, is a yearlong program, taking you from your first tentative decision to become a runner (reflected, perhaps, by buying this book) to the point where you're running somewhere between 1 hour and 2½ hours a week. Your midterm assignment is to find half a dozen pleasant running routes in your neighborhood. The final exam is to review your progress at the end of the year and identify the ways in which your health, fitness, confidence, and ability to manage stress have improved. Mark your calendar now; you may be surprised at how much your life will have changed. You may even find that your self-image has acquired a new and unexpected component: that unfamiliar but exciting new word *athlete*.

The second part, Running 201, is titled Expanding Your Horizons to underscore the fact that the topics it covers are optional. Don't set any of the topics as goals until after you've made the transition to being a runner, and even then do them only if they sound like fun. This section will introduce you to techniques for running farther, faster, and in new environments, ranging from fun runs to trail running and competitive road racing. For those who are so motivated, much of Running 201 discusses racing, up to and including marathons.

Your midterm assignment, should you choose to pursue one of these electives, is to pick a challenge that sounds like fun, set a speed or distance goal that does not unduly stretch your abilities, and work out a cautious training program for achieving your goal. The final is similar: implement your training program and have a blast at the big event itself.

SOME BACKGROUND: BOSTON YOUTH TO BOSTON MARATHON

I spent several years as one of the world's top-ranked road racers, setting a world record in the marathon at 2:08:13, making two appearances on the U.S. Olympic team, winning the Boston Marathon, and scoring three consecutive victories in the New York City Marathon. My world-record stood for nearly two decades as the fastest ever posted by an American. But like any runner, yourself included, I knew nothing about the sport before I started running seriously.

My older brother Ricardo first introduced me to the sport I would soon come to love. I was in fifth or sixth grade; he was on the high school track and cross-country teams. Together, we would organize the neighborhood kids for 50-yard dashes or longer runs around the block. I'm sure I was eager enough to beat my friends, but at the time it was just play.

A year or two later, I joined my junior high school's track-and-field team, where I did well enough that in eighth grade I was allowed to run with the high school junior varsity team for two races, which I won. There, I continued to win races without any training.

When an activity you love generates positive feedback, you tend to do more of it. Eventually, you begin seeking ways to get ever better. So it was with running and me. The difference between world-class competitors and many other runners isn't that world-class competitors are more dedicated or more willing to put in the training. Recreational runners can also be very dedicated. The difference is that elite runners receive years of positive reinforcement that encourages them to dig ever deeper for those increments of speed and endurance that spell the difference between a good performance and the best your body is capable of giving. It's that positive feedback loop that ultimately allows a few of us to make running into our careers.

For me, that process truly began in high school, where as a freshman I was the best runner on the cross-country team and league champion in the 2-mile. After winning several state high school championships, I went to the University of Oregon, where as a junior I qualified for the 1980 Olympics in the 10,000-meter. Unfortunately, that was the year the United States boycotted the Moscow Olympics, so I was unable to compete. Instead, I entered the 1980 New York City Marathon.

I had always considered the marathon to be my ultimate calling. You can't grow up near Boston without taking an interest in the Boston Marathon. My childhood home was only 3 miles from the race's midpoint, and my brother and I used to line up to watch it every year. During my junior year in high school, I started running with the Greater Boston Track Club, most of whose members were former collegiate competitors in their mid-twenties. One was Bill Rodgers, who would soon start a multiyear reign as the world's top marathoner—and at age 16 I could almost keep pace with his track workouts. That was when I set the goal: when I was old enough, I too would run marathons.

I won that first year in New York. The next year, I came back and broke the world record by 19 seconds. In 1982, I won again in New York and also survived a marathoner's worst nightmare—a sprint to the finish against Minnesotan Dick Beardsley to win the Boston Marathon by 1.5 seconds, at the time the closest Boston finish in history.

Hard Lessons Learned

Those were the glory years. In 1984, I qualified for the Los Angeles Olympics, where I was favored to win. But I had exhausted myself by training too hard, and it was hot—never my strong suit. I finished poorly, in fif-teenth place.

The next few years were even more disappointing. I was in a downward spiral of declining performance during which I exhausted myself even more by trying to push through with ever-harder training. I eventually learned that my problem was asthma, but not before that condition and my efforts to power through it had made substantial inroads on my lung function. To-day, I have only 60 percent of the lung function I had in my prime—an impossible deficit to overcome as a marathoner.

> **Only dogs and wolves
> are as well built for long-distance
> running as humans.**

But there are events where other factors are more important than lung capacity. One of these is the Comrades Marathon in South Africa, a 54-mile point-to-point course that has run annually since the end of World War I. At that distance, you can't run fast enough to get particularly out of breath, even with a diminished lung function like mine. Rather, such races are a test of how long you can sustain a more modest pace.

That ultramarathon was my farewell to world-class racing. In 1994, I won it—the first American ever to do so—in 5:38, about 8 minutes shy of the course record. Since then, with my asthma well under control, I've joined the ranks of fitness runners, putting in no more than 30 miles a week. Af-ter years of training 100 or more miles a week, I find I'm content. What I do now keeps me trim and healthy. It's good for my asthma and gives me that great feeling that comes from knowing I'm in good shape—not for compe-tition but simply to enjoy daily life.

RUNNER, KNOW THYSELF

This book is written for beginners. It's also aimed mostly at people whose running goals center around fitness, weight control, and the overall health benefits of exercise—not at those trying to eke out a few extra seconds of speed in a race. Perhaps you've chosen running as your route to fitness because it offers a way to get a good workout in a limited amount of time. Perhaps you like the fact that running shoes are a lot less expensive than a health club membership and are more portable and easier to store than a bicycle. Perhaps running is the easiest sport to do from your home or office, or perhaps you just like the fact that it's the oldest and most natural of all sports. Humans were made to run. A well-trained hunter can actually run down a deer or even a horse—although only a few remote tribes or world-class ultramarathoners still possess this skill. Only dogs and wolves are as well built for long-distance running as humans.

Most modern Americans, of course, are no longer built even for short-distance running. If this describes you, don't despair. The running program in chapter 2, Running for the Decades, is designed precisely for you. Unless you have an unusual medical condition (see pages 17–18), it should work even if you're overweight or sedentary and haven't even run around the block since childhood. The key is that the program proceeds in gradual steps that give your body a lot of time to recover from years of inactivity.

That means this book is also written for you if you've previously attempted running, only to give it up after a few weeks. Most likely, your failed program was too aggressive. Stick to the one in chapter 2, without try-

Alberto (left) and Rick (right) on a winter jog in Beaverton, Oregon.

ing to achieve everything overnight, and you will be much less likely to get a sore knee or simply burn out. If there is a single guiding philosophy to this book, it is that it's better to set modest, achievable goals than to aim so high that you're always getting hurt or skipping workouts because of lack of time.

It shouldn't matter whether you're fast or slow, thick or thin, young or old. This program is built on the number of minutes spent running, not on speed or distance. By allowing your body to find its own speed, this approach automatically accounts for your specific body type.

That said, this book is still for you if you have dreams of someday trying your hand at racing. But first, you need to take your prerequisite, Running 101. Take a moment to lace up your shoes and prepare yourself to embark on a course with the potential to revise not only your health but your energy level and the depths of your very self-image. Your life may never be the same again.

Another Perspective

The advice in this book is drawn from my years of racing experience, from what I've learned as a coach of both world-class and high school runners, and from the easy-on-beginners training program I've developed since retiring from racing. Rick Lovett, with whom I've written this book, brings his own experience plus a background much closer to the average reader's. Rick tells me he's never won a race with more than 10 entrants—and never expects to. But he is a serious recreational runner who runs for fun, fitness, and sport. I've drawn on that background to complement my own view from the front of the pack.

From the moment Rick and I met, we discovered that we think remarkably alike, partly because we share a common joy in a sport that has given much to each of us. Throughout the book, you'll find sidebar advice from Rick's own experience as a fitness runner and road racer who must fit his running into a sometimes-hectic work and business-travel schedule. We met when Rick returned to running as a way to control his weight and cholesterol after an injury layoff sent him on a decade-long foray into other sports, most notably cycle touring and backpacking. Today, having shed 55 pounds of middle-age weight creep, he runs 20 to 30 miles a week, wins occasional age-group awards in local races, and continues to enjoy the active life of an outdoor and adventure-travel writer.

RUNNING
FOR FUN
AND FITNESS

AN OFT-QUOTED PROVERB says that a journey of 1,000 leagues begins with a single step. That's remarkably appropriate for running because you are literally setting out on a long journey—but one you'll conquer in such small stages that your first outings won't involve much more than a quarter-mile of running.

The goal of Running 101 is to help you start that journey in such a natural and gradual manner that by the end you'll be able to run 6 to 20 miles a week with no more perceived effort than in your first tentative forays around the block. After that, you'll literally traverse the proverbial 1,000-

league journey every three to ten years (a league is 3 miles). In a lifetime you can easily run far enough to circle the world, with mileage to spare! And it all begins, as the program in chapter 2 will make clear, with a mere three minutes of running per day.

The yearlong course that makes up Running 101 starts when you head out the door for your first lap around the block. By the course midpoint, you may be covering more than two miles per outing (actual distance will vary, depending, among other things, on your speed). Your midterm assignment is to locate several pleasant running routes near your home, office, health club, or other convenient starting points. It's an assignment you may have to repeat several times as your workout distances increase. Try to find at least a half dozen routes to give you enough variety to preclude boredom.

The final exam is, if anything, even simpler. Keep a training diary as described on pages 48–49 and use it to review your accomplishments at year's end. Be sure to be at least occasionally aware of the intangibles—overall energy level, enthusiasm, and outlook—mentioned on pages 3–4. By the end of the 12-month program you'll have achieved the goal of this book simply by improving your physical fitness, but you may well find that this is accompanied by unexpected boons in other areas of your life.

WELCOME TO THE NEW ERA OF RUNNING

IF YOU'VE READ THIS FAR, you're probably fairly serious about taking up running. But you may have doubts: Can I do it? How can I find time? How tough will it be? Is it really worth it?

These are good questions. Entering into an exercise program without asking them is like all those well-intentioned New Year's resolutions everyone makes, breaks, then makes again the next year—eventually becoming totally disillusioned. If you don't ask, you're at risk of overcommitting, failing, and persuading yourself that running is for people who are somehow "better" than you.

That would be a shame because nothing could be farther from the truth. The key to making a commitment you can keep is to be realistic. It also helps if you ease your way gradually into a program that advances slowly enough to leave you eager for more rather than dreading each workout. This approach also keeps your time commitment manageable: it's a lot easier to find a few minutes a day for a simple, basically pleasurable workout than to try to arrange your life around a training routine that only a masochist would love.

Chapter 2 presents an example of a realistic training regimen, one that begins with brief six-minute workouts that should fit anyone's schedule. But before starting to run, it pays to remind yourself of the reasons running is good for you. Even in the most humane training program, there will be days when you have to prod yourself out the door.

The best-known benefits are to your heart. Increasingly, scientific meetings of such organizations as the American Heart Association are devoting time not only to the long-understood link between diet and cardiovascular health but to the benefits of exercise. The research on this subject is now so voluminous it could easily fill an entire shelf of books. Even if you're overweight, these scientists have concluded, it's better to be active. The terms *fit* and *fat* have become opposites in contemporary culture—but the research disagrees. Obviously, it's healthier to be lean. But if you have to choose, being active may be more important than shedding a few pounds—and, of course, the activity itself may help you cut the weight.

There are several reasons for the cardiovascular benefits of exercise. To begin with, exercise trains the heart, just as it does any other muscle. The fit heart pumps more efficiently, allowing it to pump the same volume of blood with fewer beats. Ironically, elevating your pulse rate during exercise reduces your resting heart rate so much that the total number of beats a day is diminished. That gives your heart more rest, making it inherently stronger. As a by-product, exercise lowers blood pressure, reducing the risk of stroke and eliminating the need to take blood pressure medications.

Running also helps develop the system of small arteries that provide blood to the heart muscles. If coronary heart disease clogs some of these arteries, the others would be better able to compensate. This doesn't make you immune to heart attacks, but it does help reduce the risk.

The biggest benefits, however, occur in the blood itself. There are two types of cholesterol, so-called "bad" LDL cholesterol, which accumulates in artery-clogging plaques, and "good" HDL cholesterol, which acts like a chemical vacuum cleaner, sucking LDL away from vulnerable artery walls. Shifting to a low-fat diet helps lower your LDL. That alone won't raise your HDL level, but for reasons that aren't well understood, exercise does.

The long-term effects of exercise on cholesterol levels are dramatic. A recent study in the journal *Circulation* (the scientific journal of the American Heart Association) used two different measures of artery-wall health to compare exercisers and sedentary people over a wide range of ages. The researchers found that the artery walls of 65-year-olds with long histories of running or other vigorous exercise were in as good condition as those of sedentary people less than half their ages. The same artery wall improvements that help stave off heart attacks, incidentally, also help reduce the risk of stroke and can improve blood circulation in the peripheral arteries of the arms and legs. This improved circulation can be particularly helpful for some older people.

RICK'S SUCCESS STORY

Like most elite runners, I was always thin during my racing career. Now, in my early 40s, I weigh 16 pounds more than in my racing days, but at 160 pounds and a height of 6'1", nobody would call me heavy. Rick, however, has had to fight a tendency to put on weight during middle age, with unpleasant effects on his cholesterol. Here's what he has to say.

"I've never been sedentary, but when I turned 45, I was alarmed to learn that my total cholesterol had hit 241. My LDL was 160—somewhat on the high side—and my HDL was 40—revealing my family's genetic predisposition toward low HDL even though I was active as a hiker, backpacker, and bicyclist. My blood pressure was 160/90.

"A year later, I'd dropped 55 pounds, substantially increased my all-around exercise level, and returned to running. My total cholesterol was 183; my LDL was 106, and my HDL had increased to 63. My blood pressure was 120/70. Nearly as astoundingly, my resting pulse rate had fallen from 65 to 70 beats a minute to under 50.

"I'll probably never know whether it was running, weight loss, or exercise in general that produced this remarkable success, but they're all related. Multisport exercise accelerated the weight loss, while also curbing my appetite (and giving me something to do when otherwise I might have been tempted to eat things I didn't need). Running has played its greatest role in keeping me from regaining the weight, and the weight loss made it easier and a lot more fun to run."

Beyond these benefits, exercise is good for a wide range of health conditions. Diabetics, for example, benefit from exercise, partly because it helps counter their tendency to put on weight, but also because the activity helps balance their blood sugar levels. Exercise also helps prevent osteoporosis, a loss of minerals that makes bones brittle, particularly in postmenopausal women. Running appears to help counteract this process because the pounding of each stride encourages the body to strengthen the bones. Walking helps, too, but not as much. Non-weight-bearing exercises generally don't increase bone density.

Many of these benefits have been known for years, but the research continues to mount, with new studies reported almost weekly. Basically, exercise is probably good for whatever ails you—or might ail you as you grow older. To date, the U.S. Surgeon General has decided that there is sufficient scientific proof to officially identify nearly a dozen major benefits conveyed by exercise. Specifically, the Surgeon General has found that regular physical activity

- reduces the risk of premature death
- reduces the risk of heart attack
- reduces the risk of developing diabetes
- helps prevent the development of high blood pressure
- reduces blood pressure in those whose pressure is already high
- protects against colon cancer
- helps control weight
- builds strong bones, muscles, and joints
- improves the strength and balance of older adults, reducing bone-breaking falls
- combats depression and anxiety
- promotes overall psychological well-being

The fit heart pumps more efficiently, allowing it to pump the same volume of blood with fewer beats. That gives your heart more rest, making it inherently stronger.

WHY RUNNING?

Running isn't the only form of exercise that can benefit your health. But it is one of the most convenient, and it's a fairly intense exercise, compared to walking, bicycling, or gardening. Some health benefits can be obtained from any form of exercise, but others result if you elevate your heart rate to about 115 to 140 beats a minute, depending on your age. It's hard to do that with gardening. Also, the bone-strengthening effects aren't as pronounced with nonimpact sports, and if your goal is to lose weight, you'll do so with fewer minutes of exercise performing an intense sport such as running.

HOW MUCH SHOULD I RUN?

How much you should run depends on your goals. For basic fitness, the U.S. Centers for Disease Control and Prevention and the American College of Sports Medicine recommend at least 30 minutes of moderate-intensity physical activity on most days. If you want, you can get most of this by running, although your risk of injury goes up significantly if you run more than five days a week. But you can get most of the benefits by running as little as 20 minutes an outing, three days a week, and supplementing that with walking, bicycling, or any similar activity, even if it's not quite as intense.

If you want to run marathons, of course, you'll need to run a good deal more than the minimum. We'll discuss that in more depth in the second part of this book. But targeting 30 minutes per outing is plenty if health and fitness are your basic goals, especially if your overall lifestyle provides at least a modicum of other activities.

STAGES OF LIFE

There's no such thing as a "typical" beginning runner. Some people start in their 20s, when—a few years out of school—they realize that their once-active youths have faded to memory. Others are middle-aged, seeking the best possible health in years to come. Running can benefit you when taken up in almost any stage of life.

Running and Pregnancy

Late in pregnancy might not be a convenient time to begin a running program, but most women can probably run up to the last month or two before giving birth. It's important, though, to consult your doctor before doing so. Some specialists have expressed concern about oxygen deprivation to the fetus if you run too hard, but there are women who have run world-class for the first three or four months of pregnancy with no harm to their babies. Others have run recreationally right up to the last moment, with no ill effects to themselves or their children.

The main concern is your own comfort due to the increased weight and the effect on your balance. If running becomes unpleasant, shift to a non-weight-bearing activity such as swimming. You'll be able to return to running more quickly if you find some way to get in 20 minutes of exercise three times a week to slow the rate at which you lose cardiovascular conditioning (see page 155).

Children and Teens

Study after study has shown that regular exercise is as important for children as it is for adults—and that today's children are more inactive than ever. This lack of activity even carries over to school physical education programs: one depressing study found that schoolchildren often receive only a few minutes of actual exercise in their PE classes; the rest of the time is spent teaching them skills, such as fielding a baseball or dribbling a basketball, rather than encouraging them to work hard enough to elevate their heart rates.

Nevertheless, kids are generally more fit than adults, simply because they haven't yet learned to drive. That means they can definitely accommodate the running program presented in this book, at least as long as they're not severely overweight. There are a few limitations, however: no child under age 14 should run farther than 10 or 12 miles (not exactly a severe constraint for fitness running), and no growing child, even an older teenager, should run a marathon. But even a six-year-old could do the program in this book without difficulty. In Africa, children as young as age 8 run 5 miles each way, to and from school. Some grow up to be world-class marathoners.

The program in this book, in fact, is very conservative for children. High school cross-country runners generally go in a matter of months from nothing to 3 or 5 miles of running a day. Kids' joints are simply more resilient than adults', and children progress much more quickly aerobically than their parents. Training budding track stars and cross-country athletes, however, is beyond the scope of this book.

Seniors

Many people have successfully taken up running during their retirement—occasionally with inspirational success. Here in Portland, Oregon, for example, Mavis Lindgren began running in her early 60s, ran her first marathon at age 72, and by age 93 had run 76 marathons!

The program in this book is gradual enough that it really doesn't matter what age you are. It's based on time spent running, not on distance covered, and runners of all abilities are encouraged simply to run whatever pace feels comfortable. Older runners will merely run a bit more slowly than people a generation younger. But there's no reason that they, too, can't build up to 20 or 30 minutes a day.

There's no such thing as a "typical" beginning runner. Running can benefit you when taken up in almost any stage of life.

BEFORE YOU START

Before taking up running, there are two important caveats. The first is to spend some money on your feet. You could probably get away with wearing cheap shoes at the start, but you're going to need real running shoes soon enough. Buying them at the outset is a good way to commemorate your decision to become a runner—and it's better to buy good shoes early in the process than to regret not doing so later on. See chapter 4 for specific advice on shoe buying.

Second, athletic books of all kinds advise beginners to check with their doctors before setting forth on any program of vigorous exercise, particularly if you're over age 40. Consider yourself so advised. Most people, on the other hand, rarely follow this advice. That's your choice. But you absolutely should talk to your doctor if you know you have a physical condition that might preclude running or at least require monitoring. Such conditions include the following.

- *A known heart condition.* The running program in this book may be exactly what you should do, but you need medical supervision and advice geared to your condition.
- *Chest pain or a family history of heart disease.* In general, running is good for the heart, but the stress of starting a program can trigger an attack. Find out where you stand before you begin.
- *A history of amenorrhea.* If you are a woman who at any time in your life missed six or more periods (when not pregnant) due to illness or an eating disorder, you shouldn't run without first determining if you

need a bone-density scan. Hormonally, your medical history mimics early menopause, and the condition may not have been dealt with properly at the time. Without the right treatment now, you are at risk of an endless succession of the hairline bone cracks called *stress fractures* (see pages 31–32). Once the condition is stabilized, however, you may indeed benefit from running.

- *Asthma.* This is a topic about which life has chosen to make me an expert. Asthma isn't yet on the Surgeon General's list of conditions proven to be improved by exercise, but the latest medical literature strongly indicates that many asthmatics indeed benefit from running. Before you start, however, you need to make sure that your asthma is properly medicated and well under control.

- *High blood pressure.* Running can help you control your blood pressure if it is high, but you need medical advice before you start. If you haven't had your blood pressure checked recently (within the past six months), you can get an adequate reading from one of the automated machines sometimes found in drugstores or other public places.

- *Any other medical condition that raises questions in your own mind.* Ignorance is not bliss. It's better to ask your doctor unnecessary questions than to endanger your health by not asking the questions you should. Most doctors are well aware of the benefits of exercise and aren't apt to discourage you unnecessarily.

Running for the Decades: A Conservative Program for Lifestyle Running

Most people envision running as a succession of grueling workouts in which you're constantly pushing yourself to go farther and faster. The idea is that you have to do a lot of running, and it's got to be uncomfortable. It's a popular notion, even among runners. But it reflects an attitude rooted in the first running boom, where everything centered on racing—and quick success in racing, at that. For fitness runners, nothing could be farther from the truth. Intense workouts aren't necessary for reaping the benefits of basic cardiovascular fitness. What matters is consistency. The key to consistency is building up slowly enough that you want to keep doing it—slowly enough also that you don't set yourself back with an injury in the first few months. Even if racing is your long-term goal, it's useful to start slowly and lay a good foundation. Dedicate your first year to making the conversion from nonrunner to runner. Then, if you want, you can safely set additional goals for competition or heightened fitness.

This chapter presents a program for making that transformation so gradually it will probably feel almost too easy. But why suffer if you don't need to? Your goal should be to become fit, but not to do so overnight. Seeking overnight fitness, in fact, is a recipe for an overuse injury that can leave you no better off three months into your program than you were when you started—worse off, in fact, because having tried once and failed, it will be psychologically harder for you to start over again. Much as you might wish otherwise, no exercise program can be an instant fix for years of not exercising; your exercise program should be part of a healthy lifestyle whose benefits play out over the rest of your life. There's no reason not to take a few extra weeks to reach that goal as easily and safely as possible.

You probably have friends who have started running programs much more quickly and have gotten away with it. Many people can indeed do this. The problem is that you can't tell in advance if you're one of them. If you aren't, your first inkling will probably be an overuse injury, typically coming on just about the time you're really beginning to enjoy your new lifestyle.

A TOO-FAMILIAR TALE

Tempted to try to accelerate the first few months of the program? Consider the following story that Rick recently collected.

"A friend's sister took up running at about the time Alberto and I started work on this book. 'For the first month, she just walked,' my friend said. 'Then I got a call from her a few weeks later, excited because she was now running 2 miles a day. A month later, she strained something in her knee and had to lay off.'

"That's such a familiar refrain that I wasn't particularly surprised. The goal of this chapter is to help keep you from joining the same chorus."

Your beginning program should start with an easy combination of running and walking, then build slowly but steadily. After a year, you'll be running a continuous 20 to 30 minutes a day, three to five times a week, which is all that you need for fitness and is also a substantial base for progressing into racing, if that's your ultimate goal.

Some running books advise making a 10-percent increase a week, but that's far too much for *anyone* to sustain week after week after week. The key to long-run, injury-free success is a slower buildup, spread over more time. Even so, you will see a substantial amount of increase over the course of a year. The program in this chapter, for example, increases your running by a factor of 8 over the course of a year. If you were to increase by 10 percent a week for an entire year, you'd double your workload every seven weeks, expanding it by a factor of nearly 200 by year's end. Obviously, that's absurd. Programs that advocate weekly 10 percent increases are trying to jump you up to 20 or 30 minutes a day quickly, then hoping you won't break down once you get there.

The initial stages of training can be compared to taking a prescription antibiotic. If your doctor prescribes three pills a day for ten days, would you expect to kill the infection in half the time on six pills a day? Not likely. Why then, do so many beginners think that "whipping" their bodies into shape is better than building up gradually?

Not that I'm the poster child for practicing what I'm now preaching. In my racing days, I measured "fitness" by the number of miles I logged a week, and I felt "unfit" if it was less than 100 to 110. To some degree, that's necessary to perform at the elite level. But my career, good as it was, might have lasted longer if I had been less driven about logging mileage for the sake of mileage. I'd certainly have fared better in the 1984 Olympics. So, when I preach the benefits of gradual training, view me as the reformed alcoholic warning of the dangers of overindulgence. Unfortunately, as they used to say, "Been there, done that."

In my racing days, in fact, I was often criticized for working too hard. Now, I'm a firm believer in taking the long-term view: it's better to train too gradually than to overdo it. I've done training routines when every outing meant excruciating pain—buying into the notion that "good" training has to be uncomfortable. But that's just not true. All you really need to be is consistent. So, if you have the onetime "king of training" telling you it's OK to take it easy, you should believe it. It's not as though I haven't learned it the hard way.

Don't skip the walking part of your early workouts, even if you feel as though you could run the entire distance. The running-walking combination is necessary because you need to train two different bodily systems: cardiovascular and musculoskeletal. The two systems progress at different rates, with different training needs. Your cardiovascular system (and your muscles) progress rapidly, but bones, tendons, and ligaments need time to adjust to the jarring impact of sustained running and shouldn't be subjected to lengthy outings until they're ready—a process that takes several months. Your heart and lungs, however, progress most quickly from longer duration workouts. Luckily, those longer workouts don't need to be done at full intensity, so combining walking and running allows you to increase cardiovascular fitness without excess pounding. As a by-product, you'll cover more miles, burn more calories, and be less tired than you would from shorter workouts involving nothing but running.

**Seeking overnight fitness is a
recipe for an overuse injury that can leave you
no better off three months into your program
than you were when you started.**

BASIC BEGINNER PROGRAM

If you've never before been physically active—or if you haven't been so for years—your initial assignment is simply to get out running and walking for a total of 6 minutes a workout. How fast (and therefore how far) you go is irrelevant; the goal is simply to get used to jogging. Try alternating minutes of walking and slow running. That will probably feel so easy you'll almost think it's a waste of time, and you'll be tempted to leap ahead to running 10, 12, or even 15 minutes an outing. Remember, that's the fast track to injury. Remind yourself that even if your heart, lungs, and muscles can handle the stress, your bones and tendons probably can't; if you keep it up, something will eventually break down.

After a couple of weeks of 6-minute outings, you can add 1 minute of running and 1 minute of walking, for a total of 8 minutes a workout—an increment that should still feel absurdly easy. Keep progressing at this conservative rate, adding a minute each of running and walking every few weeks until, after six months, you've reached 10 to 15 minutes of each, for a total of 20 to 30 minutes. Sometime in the first few weeks, you need to decide where in this range your midyear goal lies; anything between 20 and 30 minutes is easily reachable at the start, but there comes a point where it's too big a jump to suddenly shift tracks.

During your running-walking workouts, you can continue alternating gaits at one-minute intervals, or you can gradually switch over to longer intervals of each—all that matters is the total amount of each activity. Notice that you've now at least tripled your workout but have done it so gradually that it probably still feels absurdly easy.

Now it's time to start doing away with the walk breaks. Again, the goal is to make the change very gradually, so gradually that it's going to take another six months to eliminate the breaks completely. Don't increase your daily running quota by more than a minute per workout every few weeks. And don't suddenly shift from a 20-minute workout to 25 or 30 minutes unless you do so by adding walking time only. If your running-walking workout at the six-month mark was 20 minutes, you're on track for 20-minute runs at the one-year anniversary. You can build that up to 25 or 30 minutes later on, but right now you need to concentrate on making the transition from runner-walker to runner.

Why 20 Minutes?

You may have heard that cardiovascular fitness improves most rapidly if you get at least 20 minutes of exercise per workout. That's true. Shorter-duration

ONE-YEAR TRAINING PROGRAM FOR BUILDING UP TO 20-MINUTE RUNNING WORKOUTS

Weeks	Total Time per Workout	Running	Walking
1–3	6	3	3
4–7	8	4	4
8–10	10	5	5
11–14	12	6	6
15–17	14	7	7
18–21	16	8	8
22–25	18	9	9
26–28	20	10	10
29–30	20	11	9
31–33	20	12	8
34–35	20	13	7
36–38	20	14	6
39–41	20	15	5
42–44	20	16	4
45–46	20	17	3
47–49	20	18	2
50–51	20	19	1
52	20	20	0

ONE-YEAR TRAINING PROGRAM FOR BUILDING UP TO 30-MINUTE RUNNING WORKOUTS

Weeks	Total Time per Workout	Running	Walking
1–2	6	3	3
3–4	8	4	4
5–7	10	5	5
8–9	12	6	6
10–11	14	7	7
12–13	16	8	8
14–15	18	9	9
16–17	20	10	10
18–19	22	11	11
20–21	24	12	12
22–23	26	13	13
24–25	28	14	14
26–27	30	15	15
28–29	30	16	14
30	30	17	13
31–32	30	18	12
33–34	30	19	11
35	30	20	10
36–37	30	21	9
38–39	30	22	8
40	30	23	7
41–42	30	24	6
43–44	30	25	5
45	30	26	4
46–47	30	27	3
48–49	30	28	2
50–51	30	29	1
52	30	30	0

workouts are over before you get the full cardiovascular benefits. Running, you can't leap instantly to 20 minutes a day, but if you want to speed your progression toward cardiovascular fitness, feel free to add extra minutes of brisk walking. Just don't use that as an excuse to ramp up the running more quickly than the schedule permits. Basically, you can walk all you want, but the running should still be the amount recommended in the charts on pages 23–24. Nor for basic fitness do you need to run more than three 20-minute workouts per week. Yes, public health authorities recommend half an hour of exercise a day on most days (see page 15) but not all of that needs to be from running. As your fitness improves, you'll find yourself increasingly likely to walk rather than drive, more willing to substitute stairs for elevators, and generally expanding your activity level in countless minor ways.

How Often Should I Run?

So far, we've discussed the program solely in terms of daily workouts. But how many times a week you run is also important. The optimum is somewhere between three and five days. If you only run once a week, you'll never progress. Two workouts a week might produce some increase in fitness, but it's below the medical recommendations for cardiovascular health—and you'll probably find that you're often stiff and sore afterward. Your body needs the regularity of at least three workouts a week. More than five, however, is destructive. Top-level racers train more frequently than that, but they're trying to walk a tightrope between maximum performance and injury—and all too often they err on the side of injury. Rest is as important as regularity, and there's no reason for the average runner to run more than five times a week. If you want more exercise than your running program is giving you, add another sport—one without pounding, such as bicycling. And try to take at least one full rest day per week.

Just as you need to decide fairly early in your training program whether your goal is 20 or 30 minutes a day, you also need to choose the number of times per week you want to run. It's easy to drop a day or two if four or five proves to be too time-consuming, but adding days midway through the program is more difficult. If you go from three to four days without changing your daily workout, for example, you increase your weekly total by 33 percent—a huge increment.

That doesn't mean you *can't* increase the number of days you work out. Once you've reached your one-year goal, you can phase in another day, just as you might any other additional mileage (see chapter 11 on race training). And, as the next section will describe, you have a good deal of flexibility to shift workout minutes from one day to another—even to the extent of dividing the 90 minutes of a thrice-weekly 30-minute workout into four 20- to 25-minute days, or visa versa.

BEYOND THE BASICS

The basic program outlined above is all you need to reach your ultimate fitness goal. But it needn't be as rigid as the charts on pages 23 and 24 make it appear. This section will discuss how to restructure the program to give you greater schedule flexibility and the option to run farther on days when the sun is shining and you feel fit and full of energy. It's even possible to take in an occasional 5-kilometer fun run, if that's one of your goals, fairly early in your training.

The key to a more flexible schedule is to shift your thinking from daily workouts to weekly totals. That means that if you feel sluggish today or the weather's miserable, you're free to postpone a few workout minutes until tomorrow. On the other hand, if you feel great, you can extend your workout by "borrowing" minutes from the future.

Within reason, you can also trade walking and running minutes between days. This allows you to challenge yourself occasionally by running a longer sustained distance than usual and making up for it by doing more walking and less running on another day. Injuries generally come not from the duration of individual workouts but from the workouts' cumulative effects, so unless you start trying to pile up most of your mileage into one or two days, none of these schedule shifts should increase your injury risk. If you overdo it, though, you will probably get sore muscles.

If you're looking for a rule of thumb, figure that you're OK if your longest workout isn't much more than 50 percent higher than the daily average.

The main constraint on your ability to shift minutes among workout days is the need to avoid undermining the regularity of your workouts. If your weekly schedule becomes too asymmetrical, it will feel too much like you're running only once a week. Remember also that your ultimate goal is at least three workouts of 20 minutes or longer a week. That means you have more schedule flexibility if you're working out 90 or 120 minutes a week than if you're only doing 60. One 40-minute workout and two 10-minute workouts just aren't the same, cardiovascularly, as three 20-minute workouts. But three 25-minute workouts and one 45-minute workout are cardiovascularly equivalent to four 30-minute workouts.

The following chart uses the daily workout program in the charts on pages 23 and 24 to calculate weekly totals for runners seeking to build up to anything from 60 to 150 minutes a week. If you're on the 60-minute schedule, you should shift mileage among running days only when neces-

WEEKLY WORKOUT TOTALS
For Training Programs Building Up to 60–150 Minutes/Week

Week	Target Weekly Running Time							
	60 min.[1]		80 min.[2]		120 min.[3]		150 min.[4]	
	R[5]	W[5]	R	W	R	W	R	W
1	9	9	12	12	12	12	15	15
2	9	9	12	12	12	12	15	15
3	9	9	12	12	16	16	20	20
4	12	12	16	16	16	16	20	20
5	12	12	16	16	20	20	25	25
6	12	12	16	16	20	20	25	25
7	12	12	16	16	20	20	25	25
8	15	15	20	20	24	24	30	30
9	15	15	20	20	24	24	30	30
10	15	15	20	20	28	28	35	35
11	18	18	24	24	28	28	35	35
12	18	18	24	24	32	32	40	40
13	18	18	24	24	32	32	40	40
14	18	18	24	24	36	36	45	45
15	21	21	28	28	36	36	45	45
16	21	21	28	28	40	40	50	50
17	21	21	28	28	40	40	50	50
18	24	24	32	32	44	44	55	55
19	24	24	32	32	44	44	55	55
20	24	24	32	32	48	48	60	60
21	24	24	32	32	48	48	60	60
22	27	27	36	36	52	52	65	65
23	27	27	36	36	52	52	65	65
24	27	27	36	36	56	56	70	70
25	27	27	36	36	56	56	70	70
26	30	30	40	40	60	60	75	75
27	30	30	40	40	60	60	75	75
28	30	30	40	40	64	56	80	70
29	33	27	44	36	64	56	80	70

				Target Weekly Running Time				
Week	60 min.[1]		80 min.[2]		120 min.[3]		150 min.[4]	
	R	**W**	**R**	**W**	**R**	**W**	**R**	**W**
30	33	27	44	36	68	52	85	65
31	36	24	48	32	72	48	90	60
32	36	24	48	32	72	48	90	60
33	36	24	48	32	76	44	95	55
34	39	21	52	28	76	44	95	55
35	39	21	52	28	80	40	100	50
36	42	18	56	24	84	36	105	45
37	42	18	56	24	84	36	105	45
38	42	18	56	24	88	32	110	40
39	45	15	60	20	88	32	110	40
40	45	15	60	20	92	28	115	35
41	45	15	60	20	96	24	120	30
42	48	12	64	16	96	24	120	30
43	48	12	64	16	100	20	125	25
44	48	12	64	16	100	20	125	25
45	51	9	68	12	104	16	130	20
46	51	9	68	12	108	12	135	15
47	54	6	72	8	108	12	135	15
48	54	6	72	8	112	8	140	10
49	54	6	72	8	112	8	140	10
50	57	3	76	4	116	4	145	5
51	57	3	76	4	116	4	145	5
52	60	0	80	0	120	0	150	0

[1] Equivalent to 20 minutes three times a week.

[2] Equivalent to 20 minutes four times a week.

[3] Equivalent to 30 minutes four times a week.

[4] Equivalent to 30 minutes five times a week.

[5] **R** = running; **W** = walking

sary. On the 150-minute schedule, however, you may enjoy the variety you get from a diversity of workout lengths—particularly since you're running five times a week. And you will be getting enough total exercise that you won't suffer cardiovascularly if a few workouts are shorter than 20 minutes.

FUN RUNS

Doing a fun run is similar to shifting workout minutes from one day to another. Even if it produces a sharp spike in your running total for the week of the event, a single-day challenge is unlikely to hurt you unless you've already pushed yourself to the edge of breakdown. And these runs are such great fun—and such wonderful workout motivators—that there's no need to deprive yourself. Do them with the same run-walk pattern you use on your daily workouts; many other runners will be doing the same.

KEN BAILEY/CAMDEN HERALD

You're ready for a fun run as soon as you're confident that you can cover the distance (generally 5 kilometers, or 3.1 miles) running or walking. But you'll probably be more satisfied if you can run at least halfway. That means you should have built up to at least 20 minutes of walking and jogging on your average workout. When doing the fun run, make sure you keep the percentage of walking the same as in your normal workout. For example, if you're normally walking 10 minutes and running 10 minutes, you should spend half your time in the fun run walking rather than running. If you're walking 5 minutes and running 15, you can move at the faster pace for three-fourths of the fun run. Doing this, the event may take you 40 minutes or longer to finish, but doubling your normal workout in this fashion once in a while is highly unlikely to hurt you. Don't try anything longer than a 5-kilometer (5K) race, however, until you've reached your one-year training goal and have read chapter 11 on training for longer fun runs and races.

CROSSOVER ATHLETES

If you're already fit from another sport, such as bicycling, hiking, or cross-country skiing, you may have trouble making a sufficiently gradual conversion to running. But unless your current sport is something like basketball, which involves heavy bursts of running and leaping, your bones and joints aren't much better adapted to running than a nonathlete's are.

That said, there are nevertheless a couple of changes you can make to the program. To start with, if you're already getting basic cardiovascular training from another activity, you can drop as much of the walking as you want. You can also run continuously for the full allotted time. But this doesn't mean you can start out by running 6 minutes rather than 3, or that you can safely work up to an average of 30 minutes a day in less than a year. Sorry, but it takes that long to be sure you've given your skeletal system time to adjust.

For convenience, you may want to tack your running program onto your existing workouts, particularly at the outset when you're not running very far. You'll probably find that it feels best if you run first, then bicycle or hike afterward. Otherwise you will already be tired when you start running, and you may feel excessive jarring as the shock-absorbing muscles of your quadriceps protest. Triathletes, who have to jump off their bicycles and then run, often experience "dead" legs in the first minutes after bicycling.

REST, STRESS, AND OVERTRAINING

Exercise strengthens the body by alternately stressing it and letting it recover. For this reason, weight lifters often speak in terms of "tearing down" and "building up." A good workout actually causes microscopic damage— a collection of tiny tears and other minor abuses—to the exercised tissues.

When starting an exercise program, you notice this as fatigue, sore muscles, or "stiffening up" afterward. This is nothing serious, just the normal signs you've been working harder than usual.

The body responds by building up its defenses against these tiny injuries, changing the muscles slightly at the cellular level so they won't be quite so heavily taxed the next time. Thus, the actual strengthening process occurs not while you're working out but afterward, while you're resting. One reason not to accelerate your training too quickly is to make sure you're giving your muscles time to go through this strengthening process, rather than tearing them down faster than they can regenerate.

> **The actual strengthening process occurs not while you're working out but afterward, while you're resting.**

Tendons and bones are also living tissues, and they too respond to exercise. But they have limited blood supplies and rebuild from stress much more slowly. Tendons are stressed predominantly by repeated stretching, either on impact or when the muscles attached to them contract to launch you into each stride. If you're alert to the signs, they'll usually give a little warning when they're beginning to be overworked. Classically, an inflamed tendon feels stiff and sore in the morning or at the start of your workout, then loosens up as the day progresses, producing the illusion it's getting better. All that's actually happening is that you're stretching out the attached muscle, reducing tension on the tendon. Each morning, the tendon may be stiffer and sorer than ever, until eventually you can't ignore it.

Bones are stressed predominantly by impact. They respond by increasing their density. This is the process that helps protect you from osteoporosis, but it occurs very slowly. If your training exceeds the bone's ability to react, the eventual result will be a hairline crack called a *stress fracture*.

Stress fractures don't come from a single wrong step; the culprit is repeated jarring. I could give you a stress fracture with a doctor's reflex hammer by tapping on a bone over and over, never hard enough to hurt. Tap, tap, tap for tens of thousands of repetitions until, suddenly, the bone can take no more. When you're running, stress fractures come on similarly, virtually overnight. One day you feel as though you could run forever; the next, wham, you've got a hairline crack in your foot, shin, or hip. The best analogy is flexing a coat hanger back and forth. Do it enough times and the metal will fatigue and eventually snap. The chief difference with bones is that, given a chance, they'll protect themselves by getting stronger before anything goes wrong.

Stress fractures are what I most fear in beginners who overtrain, primarily because they give no warning. But your weak link may be elsewhere: perhaps a tendon or a ligament.

Ideally, you'll never find out.

FIRST ANNIVERSARY AND BEYOND

Once you've reached week 52, you'll graduate from runner-in-training to runner. Make sure you give yourself a hearty pat on the back when you get there. But now, when you're still starting up, you might want to record a few of your vital statistics—weight, blood pressure, cholesterol—so you can see how much progress you've made when that one-year anniversary arrives. Because these things react slowly to changes, you may see additional improvement beyond the one-year mark, particularly if you continue to lose weight.

When you reach your one-year anniversary, you will also reach a potential fork in the road. One option will be to turn to part 2 of this book and seek out the new challenges presented in Running 201. Alternatively, you may be content to maintain what you've already achieved—perhaps reserving the option to explore new frontiers at a later date. Both options are equally valid.

But meanwhile, that fork in the road is a year in the future. You have plenty of things to learn about your new life as a runner-in-training. The next chapter will focus on several important aspects of this lifestyle, ranging from how fast you should be running to how to keep out of the way of cars.

THE RUNNING LIFE

LIKE BEGINNERS IN any other sport, beginning runners normally have many uncertainties: What's the best place to run? What's the ideal way to chart my progress? What's the most comfortable way to deal with inclement weather? Some answers are obvious. You'd never dream of running down the middle of a freeway, nor would you head out the door five minutes after a heavy dinner. Others are more complex. You need to learn something about pacing, for example, to avoid turning each workout into an unnecessary gruel-a-thon. And you need to learn the ways of cars, dogs, and bicyclists to avoid unwanted altercations. But let's start with something simpler.

MORNING, NOON, OR NIGHT?

Physiologically, it doesn't matter much what time of day you choose for running. But psychologically, the time can make a great difference. Unless you're simply not a "morning person," mornings will find you fresh and energized, while evenings may see you tired from the workday and less willing to exert yourself. Also, most people's lifestyles are far less subject to interruption in the morning. Running after work, it's too easy to be sidetracked by a phone call, only to find that it's now dinnertime and that by the time your meal has digested, it's too late to run. Do that too many days in a row, and you'll suddenly realize you've gone all week without a workout.

Midday is also a good time to run if your work schedule gives you a long enough break. After all, you don't need 60 minutes to chew and swallow your food. The purpose of a full hour for lunch is to give you a substantial break from work, and despite the fact that it's physical exercise, running can provide tremendous mental relaxation. It's quite feasible to change clothes, run 20 minutes, shower, grab lunch at the office cafeteria, and return to your desk in 50 minutes—with 10 minutes left to eat. And in many careers, nobody cares if you're still nibbling when you resume work. If you're trying to lose weight, you may also find that the premeal exercise suppresses your appetite, allowing you to eat less.

As a side benefit, noontime running may allow you to accumulate a cadre of workout buddies, running from your office building or adjacent ones.

KEEP IT SLOW AND EASY

Repeat three times: beginners always try to run too fast. Beginners always, always, always try to run too fast.

Intermediate runners, incidentally, are often worse. As your fitness level starts to improve and your body begins to adjust to running, one of your

OVERTRAINING: NOT JUST FOR THE FRONT OF THE PACK

Rick runs with a group that often draws people who haven't been running very long. He's collected a number of cautionary tales about beginners' overtraining, including the following story. Unfortunately, it's not unusual.

"One man came to my running club a few times who would run substantially faster than me for the first 3 miles of a 5-mile run, then lag badly in the last 2 miles. Afterward, he told me he'd been running for a year, and that each workout seemed harder than the one before. 'Does it ever get easier?' he asked.

"I asked him how often he ran and how fast. The answer wasn't a surprise: seven days a week, always as hard as possible. It was no wonder he was gradually wearing down. I told him he'd be faster, sprier, and happier if he cut back to no more than five days a week and slowed down.

"I never found out if he heeded my advice. He dropped out of the club a couple of weeks later. Hopefully it was to relax and rebuild, but I fear he'd become a casualty of his own excessive drive."

SHOWERLESS RUNNING

In my racing days, I generally trained from my home. Now I work for Nike, which provides its employees with top-quality sports facilities. But Rick hasn't always been so lucky. Here's his solution.

"Being stuck at a Stone Age office that doesn't provide access to a shower needn't keep you from being a lunch-hour runner, as long as you have a private place to change clothes. Runner George Sheehan, also a cardiologist, wrote in one of his numerous running essays that fresh sweat doesn't produce body odor. That distinctive locker-room smell comes from stale sweat that's had time to grow a substantial crop of bacteria. If you towel dry after a run and don your office clothes again, Sheehan said, you'll be perfectly presentable throughout the afternoon.

"I took Sheehan's advice to heart for two years of lunch-hour running when I was working for a consulting firm in St. Paul, Minnesota. Nobody in the office could tell whether I'd run over lunch or not unless I told them.

"Scary things, however, can happen to your sweaty running clothes. Ideally, you need a gym locker in which to secure them while they air-dry, but you'll be lucky to have that in a workplace that doesn't provide showers. More likely, you'll need to keep your running clothes in a gym bag in your office. Make sure the bag is odor-proof, or nearby colleagues are likely to complain."

primary tasks will be to avoid turning each day's outing into a race. If you don't succeed at this, you risk being perpetually rundown, frequently hurt, and likely to drop out.

Initially, your challenge will be controlling the enthusiasm and goal motivation that naturally accompany a lifestyle-changing decision such as the choice to become a runner. In the short run, you may be willing to put up with a lot of discomfort. Then, the short run will start to become the long run, and you will begin to wonder if it's worth it. Suppose your goal is to get in shape, lose 30 pounds, and lower your cholesterol by 10 points. These are feasible long-term goals, but if you start out too strongly, you may find that after a few weeks, each run feels like torture and you've lost only 5 pounds. At that point, it's easy to go back to watching the boob tube.

If you keep your pace in check, you may not lose weight any faster, but now you will be thinking, "Hey, I've lost 5 pounds already—and it's been kind of fun. I'm sad if something makes me miss a workout." It's like investing in the stock market in the hope of making long-term gains rather than a short-run killing. You're no longer tempted to bail out if the huge gains don't materialize overnight.

How can you achieve this long-term mind-set? The main trick is to convince yourself that speed is irrelevant to fitness running. Study after scientific study has shown that as long as you achieve a moderate elevation in heart rate (see the following section), there's no such thing as running too slowly. Within a wide range, in fact, most of the health benefits of exercise are achieved regardless of what speed you run. If speed is your desire, it will come in its own time, much more pleasantly if you wait for it than if you push it. Later, if you decide to take up racing, you can add drills to increase your speed (see chapter 11), but even then, most of your running will be at a modest, feel-good pace.

HOW TO AVOID RUNNING TOO FAST

There are three basic tests for making sure your running pace isn't getting ahead of your training. The most direct—but most difficult for beginners—is to monitor how you feel day today. Your first few outings will give you sore muscles, which is normal for someone taking up a new activity. But the stiffness should begin to fade after a couple of weeks. By the time you've been running a month, you should feel distinctly better than you did during the first couple of weeks.

Second, you can count your pulse for 10 or 15 seconds at strategic times in each day's run, comparing it to the age-related maximums in the table at right. Or, you can use a heart rate monitor (see page 80) to get a continuous readout of your pulse.

Your target heart rate is the bottom end of the "cardiovascular training" range—at least 60 percent of maximum. If you're exceeding 80 percent of maximum, it's definitely time to slow down; any time you're near the upper end of the range you're working harder than needed for fitness. The ideal is in the middle, but remember, it's a fairly broad middle. If you feel like it, though, there's no reason not to test yourself occasionally with a fast run. Just don't make a habit of it.

The heart rate chart should always be viewed as a guideline, not a straightjacket. Some people's pulses are naturally a bit high; other people have to work fairly hard to get their heart rates up to what the charts view as moderate effort. These variations, however, are rarely more than about 10

HEART RATES BY AGE AND PERCENTAGE OF MAXIMUM FOR ADULTS (PER MINUTE)

AGE	100%[1]	60%[2]	70%[3]	80%[4]
20	200	120	140	160
25	195	117	136	156
30	190	114	133	152
35	185	111	130	148
40	180	108	126	144
45	175	105	122	140
50	170	102	119	136
55	165	99	116	132
60	160	96	112	128
65	155	93	108	124
70	150	90	105	120
75	145	87	102	116
80	140	84	98	112
85	135	81	94	108
90	130	78	91	104

[1] Maximum may be used to calculate levels of effort not given on the table. This level corresponds to total exhaustion. Training should never be this intense.

[2] This is the minimum level of effort needed to achieve fitness benefits in a 20- or 30-minute workout. Walkers can (and do) achieve benefits at lower exertion levels, but this is because the long duration of the activity compensates for its lower intensity.

[3] Target level for comfortable fitness training. Use as a guideline only; anything in the 60 to 80 percent range will achieve good results.

[4] Maximum exertion level recommended for fitness training. Racers will occasionally exceed this in speed training workouts, as described in chapter 11 on race training, but such high-intensity workouts are unnecessary for fitness training and can lead to overtraining and associated injuries. If you choose to do higher-intensity workouts, follow the rules in chapter 11 to minimize these risks.

beats a minute. So if you're way above or below your target, it's time to adjust your pace.

A third approach for monitoring your pace is to see if you could carry on a reasonably normal conversation while running. Most beginners can't imagine doing this, but that inability is the greatest sign that they're running too quickly. Experienced runners can, and do, chatter away throughout their runs, barely altering their phrasing while they breathe. A little breathlessness is OK, but . . . if . . . you . . . find . . . yourself . . . talking . . . like . . . this . . . you're overdoing it. And if you grunt and refuse to answer a friend's questions, you're unnecessarily close to exhaustion.

As your fitness improves, of course, you may find that you need to run a bit faster to reach your target heart rate. But that increase in speed will come naturally, simply from doing the same things you've been doing all along.

> **Repeat three times:**
> **beginners always try to run too fast.**
> **Beginners always, always, always try to run too fast.**

A Word on Overmonitoring

Monitoring your heart rate is a great training tool, but it needs to be used with discretion. I used a heart rate monitor when training for the Comrades Marathon, even taking the device with me to South Africa. On race day I started to pick it up, then changed my mind. "It's time to race now," I told myself. "Do as your body tells you."

The man who finished second behind me, South African Nick Bester, trailed me by 12 minutes at the halfway point but made up 8 minutes of that before the finish. "Why'd you let me get so far ahead?" I asked afterward.

His reply: he'd been wearing a heart rate monitor, and it had told him he was running too hard at the start. So he slowed down and let me build a large lead.

There's a lesson here that applies to everyone, not just world-class athletes. The monitor is a good guide, but what it tells you isn't perfect for everyone, every day. Run the pace your body wants to run. If on some days that means going higher than the heart rate monitor recommends, that's OK. Conversely, don't let the monitor pressure you into running uncomfortably fast. That's when you get hurt or quit having fun. But if you enjoy hard workouts, you're not likely to do yourself serious harm running at the top end of your range for a couple of outings per week. You'll pound your legs a little harder but probably not enough to matter. So do what you enjoy.

Heart rate monitors are useful tools, but some people's running personalities change the moment they start using one. Rather than seeking to enjoy their runs, they become dominated by the numbers, trying above all else to please the monitor. If that might be you, check your pulse occasionally the old-fashioned way and forget the gadgetry.

Thoughts on Pain

It's an image that haunts many a middle-aged baby boomer, particularly men raised in atmospheres of too much machismo. An overweight PE coach—a football player gone to seed—looms over you as you stand, sit, or lie gasping on the floor. "It's gut check time, sonny," he says in his best drill-instructor voice. "No pain, no gain." Then you wake up in a cold sweat, go outside and hammer yourself to a pulp running too far too fast, trying to prove something to that ancient nemesis. Instead, you get sore muscles—maybe even an injury if you keep it up, day after day.

It's not that the PE coach was totally wrong. Some people need the "no pain, no gain" mantra to bestir themselves from their easy chairs, particularly after a hard day at the office. If we never exercised beyond our most slothful comfort zones, chances are that most of us would atrophy into total couch potatoes. The pain versus gain quandary comes when we apply our culture's prevailing "if some is good, more is better" attitude to the normal mild discomfort that comes with unaccustomed exercise. Some people drive themselves continually to the ragged edge of pain in the belief they're not doing their bodies any good if they're taking it easy enough to actually have fun.

It would be a lie, of course, to say that running is always the blissful "runner's high" about which some runners wax lyrical. You have to be able to push yourself a bit. Particularly when you're starting out, you're forcing your body to do something it's not accustomed to, and it's likely to protest. If you ever decide to take up racing, you'll find there are times when it protests a lot.

The key to success is to never push yourself so hard that the discomfort makes you want to quit. In part, this means keeping your long-term goals in mind. But it also means not trying to meet somebody else's standards. Everyone's different, and bodies progress at different rates. People also have different levels of tolerance for discomfort. Chart your progress by your own standards, and don't drive yourself too hard seeking to match somebody else, whether it's that childhood PE coach or a next-door neighbor who seems to be able to run forever without tiring.

Finally, be aware of your self-talk. That's not an admonition to "visualize success" or talk yourself into a positive mental attitude but rather a suggestion simply to listen to yourself and chart your training accordingly. It's one thing to find yourself admitting, "Well, there's a little bit of discomfort, but it's not that bad. I can last another 10 minutes, and it's definitely worth it." It's quite different to find yourself saying, "This isn't fun. I don't care about the benefits; I don't want to do it." Back off long before you reach the latter state. It's better to run 2 miles an outing and enjoy it than to burn yourself out trying to stretch your mileage.

There is also a difference between the normal discomfort of starting a new sport and the pain that signals the start of true injury. Here are a few pointers.

- Consistently pushing your training into the realm of severe discomfort is "overtraining." If you keep it up, you *will* eventually get injured.
- A sharp, stabbing pain should not be ignored. Maybe it's nothing, but maybe you've strained something. Walk home or call for a ride, read chapter 9 on injuries, and see how you're feeling a few hours or a few days later.
- Be alert to pain that persists after your run. Occasionally, you may have a minor strain that continues to give twinges for a day or two, but any muscle, bone, or tendon pain that gets progressively worse after each run is a sign you're overdoing it.
- Fatigue that progressively worsens, day after day, is a warning sign that you're tearing your body down rather than building it up. Cut back now, rather than after the inevitable injury.

WHERE TO RUN

One of running's great advantages is that unless you live in an area devoid of side streets or back roads, you can do it from your own doorstep. You don't need to drive to a gym or swimming pool, rent a locker, and change clothes before starting, only to repeat that process in reverse before heading home. This also means you have less excuse to procrastinate. You simply tell yourself it's time to get going, put on your shoes, and head out the door before the procrastination bug has time to bite.

Once you've gotten out the door, you may have several route options.

When you're choosing among them, the main factors should be safety, comfort, and aesthetics. These three criteria tend to be linked. Trying to share busy streets with traffic is not only unappealing, it's dangerous. Comfort mostly has to do with your choice of running surface; the ideal one is nice and smooth, with a little bit of give to help absorb each step's impact. Wood-chip running paths are supremely comfortable; asphalt is good; concrete is the worst. Aesthetics is a personal matter, but it often entails getting away from cars—exactly what you want for safety and, often, for the best footing.

With these factors in mind, here's a hierarchy of running options.

- *Off-road running paths, with surfaces of packed dirt, wood chips, or asphalt.* On the more rustic trails, you'll have to be alert for tree roots, rocks, and other surface irregularities that might trip you up. Asphalt paths often double as bike paths or routes for in-line skaters, who are faster than you.
- *Side streets.* This is where you're likely to do most of your running. Seek out routes that are mostly asphalt surfaced, and be alert for cars. Traditional advice is to run on the left side of the road, facing traffic. You'll need to do this if cars pass by frequently, but many roads have a hump or "crown" sloping away from the middle. Running facing traffic means you're always running on a surface that slants left, which is not good for your knees if you do it every day, mile after mile. Try running on the left side of the road when you're in the busiest traffic and varying the slant by running down the middle or the right side when it's safer. Remember, however, that safety always comes first.
- *Running tracks.* High schools, colleges, and public parks often have running tracks that are open to the public, free of charge. Whether they're made of asphalt, cinders, or some kind of artificial football-field material, they provide good, safe running surfaces. Running in circles, however, is monotonous. Furthermore, you'll be sharing these tracks with speedier athletes using them for timed workouts. Avoid conflicts by staying in the outside lane, and read the section on track etiquette on pages 180–181.
- *Sidewalks.* If you're running downtown in a big city, sidewalks may be the only places to run. But they're not very runner friendly. They're cluttered with pedestrians, parking meters, curbs, and other obstacles that force you to be constantly alert. You may also have an endless suc-

cession of stoplights. Even when you have the right-of-way, you have to be careful at road crossings to make sure you're seen by motorists accustomed to slower-moving pedestrians.

ADDING VARIETY

You don't, of course, always have to run the most convenient route. As you gain experience, you may want to spice up a too-familiar routine by driving to a park or a new part of town. Or you may want to meet friends for a social run, on weekends or after work. You and your friends can even jog across town for coffee or Saturday-morning pastries, then take a bus or cab back home.

But as a beginner, the best way to make running a consistent habit is to run from your home or office.

Running on a Treadmill

Using a treadmill is another good training option. You may have access to one at a health club. Treadmills produce less pounding than running on the roads, but they can be pretty dull unless you exercise in front of a TV or carry a personal stereo. If you're motivated, however, you can put in a surprising amount of time on them without suffering terminal boredom.

I like treadmills because they provide as good a workout as running on the road, on a surface that's at least as gen-

Treadmills are perfect for winter or bad-weather running.

tle on your knees as a wood-chip running path. When I was training for South Africa's 54-mile Comrades Marathon, I once put in a 35-mile day on a treadmill simply by listening to the radio while I ran.

Currently, I do about one-fourth of my weekly mileage on a treadmill—more in the winter, less in the summer. I could do it all that way, but I like running outdoors, and it's best to run the roads at least twice a week (if you're going to venture out at all), so your body isn't surprised by sudden shifts in running surfaces.

Speed for speed, treadmill running is slightly easier than road running. For fitness running, that doesn't matter; you'll just find that you're running slightly faster than on pavement. But if you want, you can simulate road running by setting the treadmill on a slight upgrade, about 1 or 1.5 percent.

One final piece of treadmill advice: because you're indoors, with limited air circulation, you'll probably sweat more than when you are outdoors. Your health club may have fans set up near its treadmills, but you may still want to keep a towel handy to mop away excess sweat.

TRAINING PARTNERS

If possible, seek out a friend to serve as your training partner, particularly when you're first starting. The ideal training partner is also a beginner, with goals similar to yours. That way you can support each other during the early stages of the transition from a sedentary life to an athletic one. The obligation to meet your training partner at a prearranged time is also a great motivator for those days when you need a kick in the pants to get out the door.

The run itself is also likely to be more fun with company. Having somebody to talk to makes the time pass more quickly, and the need to carry on conversation will keep both of you from trying to run too fast. You'll also get psychological support on those days when running isn't what you most want to be doing. Track coaches have long known the importance of this psychological support. That's one of the reasons high school and college track workouts are often group events. Many runners even find that their training partners become best friends, or that their training groups expand into social clubs.

The only downside to running with friends is that you may be tempted to turn your runs into races. These macho impulses can tempt road racers with years of experience to "leave their best races on the training course," and some "friends" delight in egging these people on to self-destructive behavior. Choose for training partners people with similar training paces, or agree with your training partners that you'll each run at your own speed and regroup afterward for conversation, dinner, or a beer.

A SOCIAL SPORT

Rick is a particularly gregarious runner. Your experiences may well wind up being very similar to his.

"Running for me has always been a social sport. When I worked for several years in a succession of big-city offices, I quickly accumulated groups of running buddies and resented interruptions that made me late for our lunch-hour outings. I also had weekend groups for longer workouts. Now, one evening a week is devoted to running with my club, and I'm always one of the first to arrive, just to make sure a traffic jam won't keep me away.

"None of this is particularly time-consuming. The lunch-hour running groups fitted easily into my schedule, and the other activities are simply things I do when I might otherwise be watching television. When I look back on the last two decades, I realize that running has often been central to my social life, and that I have a great many friends I'd never have made without it."

WARM-UP AND COOLDOWN

If you attend training clinics in virtually any sport, you'll hear speakers preaching about the importance of an adequate warm-up before commencing any vigorous activity. Attend a professional basketball or football game and you'll see this advice in practice as the players run through loosening-up drills in the minutes before the game. Runners often do the same thing; at large road races, you'll see the serious contenders out for warm-up jogs as the minutes count down toward the start.

A formal warm-up isn't necessary for training runs or fitness running, in which you won't be jumping instantly from a standstill to peak performance. Instead, you can incorporate the warm-up into your workout simply by not starting out too quickly. Elite runners do the same on their training runs by running much slower than normal for a few minutes until their bodies feel loose, limber, and ready to go.

least half a mile. The stitch eventually went away—but they usually do that anyway, so who knows if it worked? I wound up finishing second, which pleased me at that stage in my career. But I'm sure everybody who saw me wondered: what on earth is that guy doing holding his lip?

BELLY BREATHING

If you repeatedly suffer from side stitches even though you're running slowly and haven't eaten for hours, your difficulties may have other causes. I've never had this problem, but Rick did when he was first starting out. In the process of beating it, he learned some breath-control tricks that may work for you, too.

"Many adults have forgotten how to breathe the way nature intended. Put your hand on your stomach and watch what happens when you draw a breath. If you're breathing properly, your hand should move outward with each breath, as your belly expands. This happens because the diaphragm fills the lungs by pulling downward on them, creating suction that draws the air inward. The diaphragm's downward shift compresses the organs that lie beneath it, causing your belly to bulge outward. That's proper breathing, called 'belly breathing.' Many people, however, suck in their stomachs and throw out their chests with each breath, called 'chest breathing.' If you're a chest breather, your hand on your chest will move inward and upward with each indrawn breath.

"Chest breathing teaches you to tighten your abdominal muscles with each breath, restricting the diaphragm from fully inflating the lungs. That's no problem in daily life. But when you start exercising heavily, the diaphragm simply can't keep up. Eventually it cramps, doubling you over with a painful stitch.

"If you're a singer with training in breath control or a childhood athlete like Alberto, you've long ago conquered this problem. Otherwise, learning to belly breathe may come naturally as you become more athletic. A simple drill to help you make the transition is to bend over deeply at the waist, as if you were planning to touch your toes. Most people find it impossible to chest breathe from this doubled-over position. Lying on your back will achieve the same result. Put your hand on your stomach to ensure that it is indeed expanding with each breath, then stand up, without altering your breathing. Practice this enough times and your body will gradually learn. If chest breathing is the cause of your side stitches, the toe-toucher trick may also alleviate them. Stop running and bend over for 30 seconds, concentrating on breathing properly. The respite may be all that's needed for your diaphragm to relax."

There are times, though, when stitches don't go away in a mile or two. I had one that lasted 3 or 4 miles in my first New York City Marathon. There was nothing to do but back off a bit and wait for it to pass. Even so, it was agonizing the whole time. I also had to incorporate it into my race strategy. I was chasing Rodolfo Gomez of Mexico at the time. When the stitch forced me to ease off, I tried to encourage him to slow down too by backing off just far enough to tempt him to think he had me beaten. That way I had the greatest chance of catching him later on. The stitch eventually subsided, letting me pass him at about mile 21. But even if you win the race, running 3 or 4 miles with a stitch is no fun.

Sometimes, when I've had to race through a severe stitch, the pain has recurred for two or three weeks afterward. This meant I had suffered a minor muscle tear in the diaphragm, not just the usual spasm. It's one of the prices for driving your body hard enough for elite racing. If you're not willing to put up with it, somebody else will and will also end up ahead of you. Luckily, in training and fitness running, you can back off as far as necessary at the first sign of a stitch, saving yourself most of the pain.

TRAINING DIARIES

Keep a log, or "training diary," of your running. It needn't be fancy, just a quick record of how long you ran and how you felt. This will help you see how consistent you've been and will supplement your memory if you can't recall whether you've run three times or four this week. At least as important, it can provide valuable clues in case something goes wrong. If you get a sore knee, for example, a training log can help you remember what you were doing the week or so before it started. It may also help you spot recurring problems so you can eliminate their causes.

You can buy specially designed training diaries, but all you need is a wall calendar in a room you visit daily after your run. Jot down the time (and distance, if you like) you ran, plus anything unusual that happened. Particularly take note of any new or continuing discomforts so you can see if you need to take a few days off to stave off incipient injury.

The only downside of keeping a training diary is the temptation to schedule your workouts around predetermined goals, based on what looks good in the diary, rather than by paying attention to warning signs from your body. But this is most likely to be a problem only for elite athletes trying to duplicate onetime successes. Consulting their training diaries, they find, for example, that they'd been running 80 miles a week prior to a major victory, so they slavishly duplicate those 80-mile weeks, come what may.

For beginners, however, training diaries are crucial. You need to know what you've been doing because you simply don't have enough experience reading your body to wing it. Without the information a training diary provides, you may fall off the program one way or another—either by doing too much and getting hurt or by doing too little and failing to progress.

SHARING THE ROAD

You are a lightweight creature of flesh and bone, whose top speed is probably well below 15 miles an hour. Automobiles outweigh you by factors of 20 or more, are made of steel, and are a good deal faster. Never forget that in a conflict, you're at a severe disadvantage.

Legally, you are a pedestrian with all the associated rights and responsibilities. But from a practical perspective, your status is slightly different because you're moving a lot faster. Also, you will inherently prefer to run on the relatively cushioned asphalt of the road, instead of on the firmer, lumpier surfaces of sidewalks broken up by curbs or on concrete slabs dislodged by tree roots. This means you'll be living in closer association with cars than your slower-moving brethren, the walkers.

Since I was a teenager, I've probably done about two-thirds of my running on the roads. I've never been hit by a car, but in more than 100,000 career miles I've had a few close calls—maybe three times when cars passed within 6 inches of me and I didn't have time to jump away. On streets that are even semibusy, I always run facing traffic. Yes, that means I'm always fighting the same leftward slant to the road (see page 41), but I'd rather worry about sore knees than about cars. I'll wait for quieter parts of my course to run on flatter surfaces or ones with the opposite slant.

Running anywhere in the vicinity of cars is inherently dangerous, but it's often necessary. Here are a few tips for reducing the risk as much as possible.

- *Ditch the personal stereo.* Your ears are nearly as valuable as your eyes in alerting you to danger.
- *Avoid roads with blind corners, unless you're on a sidewalk.* If a fast-

moving car comes around the bend, you'll have virtually no time to react. If you have no choice but to travel such a road, move as far left as possible, slowing to a walk if necessary. Listen for engine noise, always assuming a car will appear at the worst possible instant. No matter how light the traffic, don't presume you can get away with running full tilt around the bend "this time," with your body hung far out into the lane waiting to be picked off. Taking chances like that will eventually catch up with you.

- *When running sidewalks, beware of alleys or driveways diving out of narrow slots between buildings.* Cars can pop out of these places at the most unlikely instants, and there's often enough street noise that you can't hear them coming. Slow down and stop, if necessary, to peer around the corner before committing yourself to crossing.
- *If a car is paused at a stop sign or stoplight, don't jog across in front of it without making eye contact with the driver.* Drivers planning right turns tend to focus their attention to the left, seeking gaps in the traffic. Even if they're trying to be alert to pedestrians, they're probably not thinking about runners. From their perspective, you'll tend to materialize out of nowhere.
- *When a car is stopped at a potential right turn, you're generally better off to go behind it rather than in front.* The next driver in line is much more likely to be looking your way. But don't shoot through narrow gaps without being aware that the front car might suddenly back up. Similarly, when crossing a parking lot, always be alert for cars unexpectedly backing out of their slots.
- *Wear bright, visible clothing.*
- *Presume all drivers are deaf, blind, and stupid.* Even if they aren't, everyone occasionally gets distracted or makes a mistake.
- *Heed the normal pedestrian rules at stoplights and other intersections.* Groups of runners on noontime or after-work jogs through big cities are notorious for bringing traffic to a halt as they violate traffic rules willy-nilly. Not only is this rude, but impatient, angry drivers are particularly dangerous.
- *Never race a car for an intersection.* Once you're out in the road and committed to crossing it, it's OK to speed across, but dashing ahead of a car is risky. You may misjudge the car's speed, or the driver may see you coming and speed up in the mistaken belief he can beat *you.* More likely, drivers are looking for slower-moving walkers, not runners, so they don't expect your sudden appearance.

- *When crossing from one side of a road to the other, as you might to catch a sidewalk or bike trail or to prepare to turn a corner, glance back at least twice to make sure no cars are coming up from behind.* It's amazingly easy to overlook something on a single quick look back, and the cars aren't going to expect you to swerve across in front of them.
- *When necessary, wait for traffic to clear.* A few seconds' pause isn't going to reduce the value of your workout. It takes longer than that for your heart rate to drop back to a level that isn't giving you health benefits. If you really don't want to miss a few seconds of work, stop your watch whenever you have to wait for a gap in the traffic or for a stoplight to change.

NIGHT RUNNING

Ideally, you should run during daylight whenever possible or move inside to a treadmill or indoor track. But most people's schedules occasionally squeeze them into nighttime workouts, particularly during the late dawns or early sunsets of midwinter. And not everyone has access to a well-equipped health club or university gym.

There are four basic rules for predawn or postdusk running. The first is to dress for maximum visibility. Make sure your clothing has reflective stripes and that these are visible not only from in front and behind but also from the side. Also good are shoes with reflective panels on the heels. From the rear, your foot motion makes these panels surprisingly eye-catching. In addition, many shoes have reflective ribbing or taping that shows up well from the side and in front, even if the stripes are only a few millimeters wide.

The second rule is even simpler: no matter how many reflectors you're wearing, assume you're invisible. If a motorist has been blinded by oncoming headlights, this may be the case. Remember, too, that you may also encounter nighttime bicyclists, who may not have headlights to illuminate your reflectors and who have a frightening ability to appear silently out of nowhere, sometimes on sidewalks or on the wrong side of the road. Don't run at night on roads unless there's very little traffic and you can easily step onto lawns or into a ditch to avoid passing cars. Even then, be prepared to yield the right-of-way to anything that moves, even if you think you've probably been seen. "Probably," in the long run, isn't good enough.

The third rule is to make sure you can see where you're going. Pick a well-lighted route or carry a flashlight, watch for low-hanging branches, and slow to a walk before risking a misstep into a chuckhole. With or without a flashlight, oncoming headlights can blind you enough that you have to stop and wait for the car to pass. Some runners make their flashlights serve double duty by pointing them at traffic, whether it's coming from ahead or behind, to make themselves that much more visible.

Finally, make sure you're running in areas where you're safe from assault or robbery. Dark alleys and bushes are particularly threatening at night.

BIKES, PEDESTRIANS, AND IN-LINE SKATERS

Bicycles and in-line skaters are threats to you. With pedestrians, the roles are reversed, and you're the one who is more likely to cause the harm.

The key to living with bicycles is not to let them startle you when they come up from behind. Courteous cyclists will announce themselves as they approach, typically by calling out, "On your left." This, or the less-common tinkle of a bell, rarely means, "Get out of my way!" It's simply to inform you of the cyclist's presence, so you're not overly startled when she whirs past. If the path is narrow, you may want to move right, but don't veer either direction until you know exactly where the bicycle is going. The cyclist's chief hope is that you'll keep moving in a steady, straight line, with no unexpected jags.

In-line skaters are a bigger nuisance because their sideways kick makes them veer back and forth across the path, taking up more room than

THE VIEW FROM TWO WHEELS

Rick bicycles several thousand miles a year and has written two books about cycling. Here's his cyclist's perspective.

"As someone who's both a runner and a cyclist, I've come to expect runners to behave improperly when I pedal up from behind. If I say, 'Cyclist on your left,' most will panic and step leftward, directly into my path. It's so common that I count on it, generally braking to jogging speed and waiting for the runners to get over their initial startlement.

"Most cyclists aren't runners. They hate slowing down for pedestrians, and they'll blame you if you veer into their paths. In cyclist speak, what they want you to do is to 'maintain your line.' School yourself to oblige them."

either you or a cyclist. Worse, they're often wired for sound and seem oblivious to the rest of the world. Cyclists hate them; you'll probably sympathize. Don't expect an "on your left" from a skater; if you're lucky, you will hear the rumble of approaching wheels. But the chief safety rule is similar to that for cyclists: don't do anything unexpected. It's the skater's job to avoid you, not yours to avoid the skater. But obviously, once you know the skater's planned path, you should yield enough room to make it possible.

With pedestrians, you're the fast one coming up from behind. Realize that you're as scary to them as cyclists and skaters are to you. Give them a wide berth, slow down, and avoid zooming by so closely you put them at even a metaphorical risk of a heart attack.

DOGS

Dogs may be man's best friend, but they aren't runners' friends. There's nothing like a snarling canine threatening to take a chomp out of your Achilles tendon to make you wonder why you didn't take up a nice tame sport like bungee jumping.

Nevertheless, dogs are a much-overrated hazard. Unless you're intruding on private property, most are harmless, barking and wagging either to announce their presence or because they want to join the fun. The dangerous ones are those that neither growl nor bark. They come straight at you without a sound and can be on you practically before you realize they're coming.

When accosted by a dog, don't even think of trying to run away. Canine instinct is to chase, and even playful dogs may try to tackle you by grabbing your heel. Furthermore, you'll never outrun the dog; even the tiny yappers can put on remarkable bursts of speed.

Your best move is to turn and confront. At that point, your attitude can range from firmly commanding the dog to "*Go home!*" to a friendlier, "Hi there, fella," though it takes experience to know which is best. You've probably been told not to show fear, but it's best not even to *be* afraid. That may sound like a tall order, but dogs sense fear and it brings out something atavistic in them, greatly increasing the threat. If *you* believe you're in control, so will most dogs. If you can't imagine not being afraid, consider this: you're capable of doing more damage to most dogs than they are to you. Visualize yourself punting that irritating critter right across the street. Self-defense books or classes can teach you how to deal with bigger dogs. You're very unlikely ever to have to react violently, but if you believe you're capable of it, the dog is likely to think so too and avoid testing your resolve.

OTHER SAFETY TIPS

Depending on where and when you run, you may have to take other precautions. Even if you're not concerned about dialing 911 to ward off a human attacker, you may want to carry a cell phone—or at least coins for a pay phone—in case you need to call for a ride. Carry the weight close to your body in a fanny pack or in the breast pocket of a running jacket, and put it in a plastic bag if you're worried about perspiration or rain.

Similar items that might be useful to have with you are public-transportation passes, a few dollar bills, and identification cards. Runners with special medical needs should carry medical alert information and any medication that might be vitally needed on short notice. If you're allergic to bee stings, for example, it's wise to carry your bee sting kit during bee season. And if you're asthmatic, have your inhaler handy.

Sportswear market researchers recently polled hundreds of runners to determine what they carried on their workouts, discovering an astonishing variety of oddments. Running apparel is now being designed to make it simpler and more comfortable to carry such items.

EXTREMES OF HEAT AND COLD

It's possible to run at temperatures as low as −40°F and as high as 100°F or more. But such extremes are dangerous unless you're extremely well prepared.

Running is generally most comfortable in conditions the average person would view as slightly on the cool side. What that means depends on the climate you're used to, but generally anything above 80°F is uncomfortably warm, while 40°F or lower is cool enough to catch most people's attention.

Heat is particularly dangerous. Acclimate to it gradually, adjusting the time of your daily runs if necessary. As a beginner, be wary of temperatures in the 80s, and avoid temperatures above 90°F unless you live in a place like Phoenix and are so well heat acclimated you view that as cool. In humid climates, even 80°F is hot.

Some people handle heat better than others. Part of the difference is related to body build; fine-boned, skinny people generally shed excess heat better than heavy people, but it's hard to predict individual reactions.

When running in warm temperatures, the fundamental rule is to take it easy and to make sure you don't dehydrate (see pages 197–98). Cut your pace to whatever feels comfortable, carry a water bottle or get a drink whenever you get a chance, and consider reducing your planned distance. You may also want to shift your runs into the early morning or evening to avoid the midday extremes and the directly overhead sunlight that can turn your running route into an oven.

A sudden feeling of being chilly on a hot day is a not-to-be-overlooked sign of significant dehydration. Stop running immediately, find water, and get out of the sun. Feeling faint isn't good, either, and difficulty in concentrating or the realization that you've stopped sweating is an indicator of potentially deadly heat stroke. (And beware: contrary to beliefs of the past, you can get heat stroke even if you never quit sweating.)

Some of these signs are hard to spot in yourself, making it particularly useful to have a training partner in warm weather.

Other hot-weather running cautions include

- shifting as much as possible to shady courses
- cutting back your running or taking the day off if smog or allergens are high—particularly if you have a medical condition that might be aggravated by them
- being particularly cautious when heat is accompanied by humidity
- warming up, stretching, and cooling down outdoors rather than going directly from a run into air-conditioning, or vice versa
- taking proper precautions against sunburn
- wearing light-colored clothing, including a mesh, billed cap to reduce the amount of heat absorbed directly from the sun
- wearing a loose-fitting shirt, tank top, or singlet that shades your skin from sun while providing maximum air circulation

Cold is often easier to deal with than heat; all you have to do is put on enough clothes. What's right will depend not only on the idiosyncrasies of your own body but also on how fast you run. Lycra running tights will serve you well at temperatures well below freezing; heavier polypropylene tights will carry you even lower. For the upper body, you'll want a Dri Fit, Capilene, CoolMax, or other warm-when-sweaty shirt (see chapter 4 for more information), lightweight gloves, and possibly a hat or earmuffs. If that's not enough, add a windbreaker, windproof track pants, and a thicker shirt. Because much of the body's heat loss is through the head and neck, a stocking cap and a skier's "neck gaiter" (a pullover neck warmer) should also be part of your winter gear, although these will cause you to overheat in any but the most severe conditions.

Cold weather carries three main risks: muscle pulls, hypothermia, and frostbite. Muscle pulls occur when chilled muscles refuse to warm up, generally because you're not wearing enough clothing. Northern runners quickly learn that this is a real risk. Make sure you start your winter runs going upwind, so the run back home is warmer than the start, in case you've dressed too lightly. In your first winter outings, be conservative until you've learned how much clothing you need in any given circumstances and stay close enough to civilization that you could get somewhere to warm up if you need to. If you've recently moved to a cold climate from a milder one, be cautious until you've fully acclimated.

Chart your progress by your own standards, and don't drive yourself too hard seeking to match somebody else's.

WINTER TRAINING

Winter is the most difficult time to run. In the summer, you can dodge the worst heat, even if you live in Phoenix, by running early enough in the morning. But if you live far enough north, winter brings unavoidable difficulties.

Snow is a greater problem than cold is. Snow is lumpy, packs into a surface nearly as hard as concrete, and can mask icy spots that can turn your run into an unintended exercise in ice-skating. Running through deep snow is also extremely hard work.

If you have no choice but to run in snow, slow down enough so you can react to uneven footing. Take particular care not to reach out too far ahead with your stride (see the discussion on pages 89–91). If you do so as you hit an icy patch, your heel will skid forward and you'll be lucky not to strain a hamstring or land on your posterior. In deep, loose snow—anything more than 2 or 3 inches—you'll have to run with an exaggerated up-and-down motion to make sure your foot comes high enough that your toes don't drag. This motion is unnatural; if you start to feel pain anywhere in your legs, take a day or two off rather than risking an injury.

If conditions outside are too miserable, your only choice is to move inside. That gives you two options: indoor tracks and treadmills.

For the average runner, treadmills are better. They simulate outdoor running nicely and provide a soft surface that's generally good for you. They're so comfortable, in fact, that when the weather moderates and you go back to running the roads, you risk sore knees if you don't phase in that change gradually, over the course of several weeks. Unfortunately, treadmills are expensive ($2,500 for a quality model) or require a health club membership.

If you hope to run on an indoor track, be prepared to do some searching. Most health clubs don't have indoor tracks—or have ones that are so short that you're always rounding sharp corners, a good way to develop sore knees or even collide with other runners. University facilities are sometimes better than commercial clubs, but generally, you have to be a student or employee to join—check with the university fitness center to find out if they offer memberships for members of the community. Some running clubs arrange special access to facilities they don't own themselves: one Minnesota club I know of obtained weekly access to the concourse of the Hubert H. Humphrey Metrodome. The surface was concrete, but it was a full two-thirds of a mile around—a big plus. If you live in a northern clime, check with local running stores for similar opportunities.

Special Frostbite Dangers

With proper equipment, you can run at temperatures that could easily immobilize a car engine. I've never run at temperatures much below 0°F, but when living in Minnesota Rick's personal limit was a chill factor below about −40°F. At that temperature his difficulty lay in finding clothing that would give him freedom of motion for running while keeping frostbite at bay. After getting "frost nip" on his ears (frostbite that penetrates no more than skin deep) through a wool stocking cap, he decided to sit out the coldest days.

Remember also that frostbite is insidious. It numbs as it freezes, so you may not be aware of what's happening until it's too late. Experienced northerners regularly flex fingers and toes and pat their faces or other cold-exposed areas just to make sure they've not gone numb. If you find a numb spot, take immediate action by rubbing the affected skin (*not* with snow, despite folklore to the contrary) to restore circulation, adding more clothing, or going indoors immediately. Numbness doesn't necessarily mean you've gotten frostbite yet, but you'll need to act immediately to prevent it.

Men should take appropriate care to avoid frostbite in the groin. In extreme conditions, tights warm enough to keep your thighs comfortable simply are not warm enough to protect the groin. Luckily, true frostbite never happened to me, but it did happen to a friend of Rick. And my entire cross-country team came so close to it at the NCAA cross-country championships one 8°F day in Spokane, Washington, that we easily understood the threat was real. We won but paid for it in the agony of warming up afterward. One solution is to stuff a spare sock into your underwear for added insulation. Or you can buy insulated "wind panel" briefs designed to protect skiers from the same risk. Or just wear several layers of underwear, which is what I did the next time I ran a frigid cross-country race.

Finally, if you live in an area where the municipality salts the roads, you need to beware of frostbiting your toes. Salted snow is liquid enough to soak your shoes at temperatures down to about 15°F, and it's easy to forget that this liquid is well below freezing. With dry shoes, however, your toes are pretty well protected. The constant flexion that comes with running spurs the blood circulation, helping to keep your toes a lot warmer than they'd be if you were merely standing around.

Not Just for Skiers

Despite the complications of winter running, it has its pleasures, too. Some cities plow the most popular running paths, providing decent surfaces even in the heart of the snowy season. Others offer winter road races or fun runs, including midnight runs on New Year's Eve that are a highlight of many runners' annual calendars. And there are few joys to match that which comes with the first light fall of powder snow. Your footsteps are whisper-light, the world is a magical place of freshly blanketed white, and if the snow wasn't preceded by rain, you know there's no ice underfoot to betray you.

Such conditions may happen only once a year, so when they do, don't hesitate: lace up your shoes and grab the opportunity for a memorable run.

HYDRATION

Even in cool weather, running generates enough body heat to work up a pretty good sweat. The lost liquid needs to be replaced as quickly as possible. Get into the habit of drinking a full 8-ounce glass of water 15 minutes before you run and immediately afterward, regardless of the weather.

There are two reasons for being fanatical about this. First, the average American drinks far too little water even for a sedentary life. If you're typical, you're likely to be beginning your runs slightly dehydrated. Second, scientific studies have shown that blood flow is better and exercise feels easier if you're fully hydrated. Why handicap yourself by not drinking enough?

Rehydrating immediately after you're finished is important because maintaining good blood flow spurs quicker recovery, translating to reduced stiffness and more energy for your next run. Elite athletes now think in terms of a 15- to 20-minute window of opportunity for taking a good drink after each outing.

If part of your running plan is to help you lose weight, be aware of the calorie content of your postworkout drink. Rick once had a friend who was exercising to lose weight but who liked to drink 32 ounces of lemonade after each workout. The liquid was good for him, but his drink contained 320 calories—about the same number you burn off in a 3-mile run. From a weight-loss point of view, the lemonade undid his workout. If you're watching your weight, stick to water or other zero-calorie beverages or adjust subsequent meals to compensate.

Sports Drinks. Top athletes usually rehydrate with a sports drink containing protein and carbohydrates. As a beginner, you needn't buy these drinks unless you want them—just make sure you get something liquid into yourself right away after the run. Beware of caffeine-containing drinks like colas or iced tea, however. Caffeine is a diuretic, which means that the fluid will go right through you, rather than be retained for rehydration.

4

EQUIPPING YOURSELF

COMPARED TO MOST OTHER SPORTS, running is inexpensive. You can start for less than $125 and outfit yourself comfortably for year-round running in any but the most severe climates for about $300. That's a lot less than you'd spend on even basic equipment for other outdoor activities, such as bicycling, skiing, backpacking, and canoeing.

The reason, of course, is that running doesn't require much equipment. Once you have shoes, socks, running shorts, and a T-shirt, you're ready to go. Add rain gear, tights, a hat and gloves, and a couple of different-weight long-sleeved shirts made of some warm-when-wet miracle fabric, and you're ready for temperatures of freezing and below. There's almost no need for high-tech gadgetry, although you may want a good sports watch and a pulse rate monitor to help track your progress.

SHOES

Shoes are your most important purchase. If there's one place not to scrimp, this is it. Unless you get lucky and find the perfect shoe on closeout, decent running shoes are going to cost about $75 to $100. Don't try to substitute inexpensive sneakers. They're made for casual walking, not for running. Even if you're running only a mile or two a day, your feet will be striking the ground far more frequently, and with much greater force, than when walking. Sneakers simply aren't designed to combat this level of stress; not only will they wear out quickly, but they'll transmit the shock of

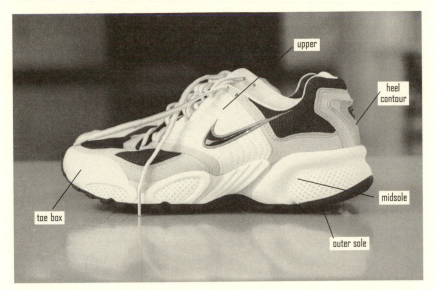

ANATOMY OF A RUNNING SHOE. This shoe has good cushioning qualities. A motion-control shoe would have a stiff heel counter, and possibly a plastic strip along the inside of the midsole, particularly beneath the arch and the heel, to prevent the shoe from rolling inward with each stride.

each footstep directly into your foot and from there up your leg to your knee and even your hip. Good shoes are the number one key to long-term, injury-free running.

All major running shoe companies make good shoes. But even within a single company's product line, not all shoes are alike—a good thing, since runners also differ widely. Nevertheless, all good running shoes combine two basic features: cushion and stability. Shoe design is inherently a trade-off between the two. A shoe with an extremely thick gel or air sole, for example, may be wonderfully cushioned, but it's also not the most stable design because all of that cushioning elevates your foot, a bit like walking on high heels. Shoes built for greater stability are lower to the ground, with wider soles that are sometimes flared. They may also contain arch supports and extremely stiff heel counters designed to keep your foot from twisting improperly with each stride. All of this, however, comes at the cost of reduced cushion—partly because there's less room for shock-absorbing materials and partly because the cushioning itself decreases the shoe's stability.

Which type of shoe you need depends on your feet and your body. If you're a big person, you'll probably need greater-than-average cushion. If your feet tend to roll inward or outward with each step, you'll need a stable "motion-control" shoe.

As a beginner, it's hard to know which type you'll need. For that reason, it's important to shop at a specialty running store, not a discount shoe warehouse. Long before I reached world-class competition, high school and college coaches helped me choose shoes. Later, shoe companies were eager to provide whatever I needed. Even the best running store can't provide custom-made shoes or know your needs as well as a coach who has spent hours watching you run, but it can do a pretty good job.

Specialty stores may have somewhat higher prices, but their expertise is well worth it. Usually, the clerks are avid runners and are well versed in the idiosyncrasies of each shoe they sell. They're also likely to be good at predicting your needs simply by watching you walk or jog across the room in different pairs of shoes. If the weather's good, they might let you test each pair by going outside for a short jog to see how they work—something a discount store would never permit. At the very best stores, the clerks will come outside with you and *watch* you jog in their suggested shoes (or watch you run on a treadmill) to see how well they accommodate your needs.

CUSTOMER SERVICE

Rick's introduction to running shoe stores was a warm one.

"In my early running years, I found a store called the Tortoise and Hare. The chief salesman was a prominent figure on the local racing scene, and the owner frequently offered free coaching to the city's largest running club. Not only were these people experts in their fields, but they gave me a great deal of individual attention, remembering the peculiarities of my feet from one purchase to another. The result was that each successive pair of shoes served my needs better than the one before. By the time I moved away, the people at the store weren't just sales clerks, they were friends. Two decades later, I still remember them fondly."

When purchasing your first pair of running shoes, wear well-used street shoes to the store. Running isn't quite the same as walking, but there are enough similarities that the clerks can get important clues about your stride from the pattern of wear on the soles of your street shoes. For subsequent shoe purchases, always bring your old running shoes with you so the clerks can determine whether the shoes had too much or too little motion control.

Here's an important shopping hint: feet swell over the course of the day and with exercise. Unless you've already gone for a morning run, the best time to buy shoes may be in the afternoon, after a day's walking has enlarged your feet to the size they'll probably be when running. It's a fine line between a perfectly sized shoe and one that will bruise toenails.

One thing not to pay much attention to is the weight of the shoe. Although there is an old rule of thumb that says each extra ounce of weight on your feet slows you down as much as 7 ounces on your back, the difference between the heaviest and lightest running shoes isn't really all that much. Hefting them by hand, the contrast might seem substantial, but with today's light, strong materials, the range is generally less than 6 ounces. That's enough to affect your pace by four or five seconds a mile in a highly competitive race, but not enough to matter in training or fitness running. And super-lightweight racing shoes typically sacrifice both cushion and stability in the search for peak performance. Far more important is buying shoes that help you run for years in injury-free comfort.

Pronation and Supination

Shoe ads often bandy around the term *pronation* as though it were some sort of runner's plague. But pronation is part of the normal foot motion. *Over*pronation is what needs to be curbed.

In normal foot motion, the foot lands on the outside of the heel, then rolls inward as the arch compresses under the stress. The foot then rebounds and rolls back outward enough that you push off for the next stride more or less from the center of the *forefoot* (the top of the foot, toward the ankle). The inward roll is *pronation*; the recovery is *supination*.

Pronation is part of the body's natural shock-absorbing system. The knees do something similar when they bend with each stride. Imagine what would happen if you tried to run with your knees locked. Not only would your stride be jerky, but the shock of each step would transfer straight up your legs into your hips and lower back. You'd be aching almost before you'd begun.

Normal pronation gives you similar benefits by letting your feet serve as additional shock absorbers. People with high, rigid arches that won't roll inward in the normal manner are among the most injury-prone runners because their bodies jar strongly with each step. If you're one of these people, referred to as *excess supinators*, the only solution is orthotics (see pages

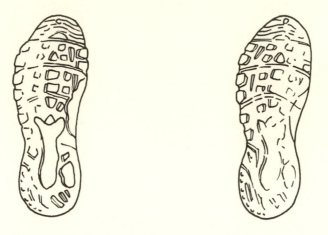

ABNORMAL SHOE WEAR. *On the left is a sole wear pattern from severe excess supination. In milder cases the heel wear may be more balanced, as in the drawing of normal shoe wear opposite, then shift too strongly to the inside. On the right is a sole wear pattern from severe excess pronation.*

83–84) and motion-control shoes designed to meet your specific needs. A trained shoe clerk can spot your problem by watching you walk or jog across the room, but the problem will also be apparent from the soles of your shoes, which will wear strongly along their outside edges, with no sign of normal pronation.

Excess pronation is more common, particularly among older runners, whose ligaments have stretched with age and no longer provide their youthful support. When the foot rolls too far inward, the effects can be disastrous all the way from the ankle to the hip because the excess pronation throws the entire leg out of line. The knees, which are intended only to flex forward and back, receive strong sideways torques, generally producing pain on their insides. But you can also get stress at the ankles, shins, Achilles tendons, and even the hips. These unnatural stresses are the single most common cause of runners' leg pains.

Overpronation has two solutions. Depending on the nature of your problem, you may need orthotics. But you can start by buying motion-control shoes designed for overpronators. As with excess supination, shoe clerks can tell if this is your problem not only by watching your stride but also by observing the wear pattern on an old pair of shoes. If you overpronate, you may strike correctly on the outside of the heel, but the wear pattern will then shift too strongly to the inside. In extreme cases, it will show that your end-of-stride *toe-off* (the point where your foot marks its final push against the ground) is all the way over on the inside of your forefoot, at the far edge of the shoe.

On the "normal" foot, the longest toe is the big toe, which is useful because this is the platform from which you launch yourself forward at the start of each stride. But a substantial minority of people have a condition called *Morton's foot*, in which the second toe is distinctly longer. These people are very likely to be excess prona-

Shoe sole wear pattern from normal or properly controlled foot motion.

tors because their undersized big toes provide too little support, reducing the ability of the foot to supinate naturally. If this describes you, make sure you tell the shoe clerk, and consider buying shoes with greater-than-average motion control. People with Morton's foot can be very good runners, but their shoe needs are often a bit finicky.

Straight and Curved Lasts

You'll frequently find claims in advertisements and running-store literature about the shoes' *lasts*. Such ads can be a bit intimidating for beginners, especially if the ads use a lot of technical talk in an effort to persuade you that the shoe represents some great new design breakthrough.

The *last* is simply the mold on which the shoe is constructed. It can be either straight or curved, giving shoes that are referred to as *straight-lasted* or *curve-lasted*.

If you're wearing shoes made for the traditional U.S. market, chances are that you're wearing curve-lasted shoes as you read this book. Look at the sole, and you'll see a distinct bend, both on the outside and the inside—the standard difference between left and right shoes that we've been taught since preschool. Many of us are so used to curve-lasted shoes that we've forgotten that this isn't actually the shape of our feet. Pull off your shoes and take a good look at your feet. Unless you've got nasty bunions, you may be surprised to realize that they're actually pretty straight. They leave curved footprints when you walk barefoot in sand, but that's because the arch doesn't fully contact the ground, not because your feet themselves are dramatically curved.

Even though curve-lasted shoes are shaped quite differently from your foot, they're comfortable because they let the arch bridge up over the edge of the shoe, hanging out a bit to the inside. But in running shoes this can cause problems for overpronators, whose arches need as much support as they can get. Straighter-lasted shoes have much less difference between the left shoe and the right shoe. To the eye of someone accustomed to wearing curve-lasted shoes, straight-lasted running shoes (and European straight-lasted street shoes) look less stable because the forefoot doesn't flare as widely to the inside, but by putting your entire foot directly above the shoe's base, they actually reduce your foot's tendency to roll inward.

> **Unless you get lucky and find the perfect shoe on closeout, decent running shoes are going to cost about $75 to $100.**

That said, there are some fine curve-lasted motion-control running shoes on the U.S. market. There are also good *quasi-straight-lasted motion-control shoes*, which have some curve to the last but not much. True straight-lasted running shoes are rare.

If all of this sounds confusing, don't worry. Although the designations at the shoe-design level can become incredibly complex and also change a bit with each year's new crop of designs, you don't need to be an expert on shoe lasts to buy good shoes. Rather, your decision should be based on fit, comfort, and the professional advice of the shoe clerk, not on an arbitrary preference for one type of last or another. Nevertheless, it's useful to know enough about the technical terms not to be too baffled when you encounter them.

"If It Ain't Broke . . ."

Uncorrected overpronation doesn't always lead to injuries. Apparently, some people's bodies adjust to the stress in ways that appear to be fully protective.

In my racing days, the standard wisdom was to leave these people well enough alone. But lately, coaches have concluded that excess pronation robs them of energy by causing them to push off in slightly the wrong direction with each step. Rather than pushing off dead ahead as they ought to, these people alternate back and forth, with a motion a bit more like a roller skater's than the perfect distance runner's.

Putting such people in motion-control shoes is controversial, however, because of the risk of creating new problems. This isn't just a concern for track stars. Motion-control shoes that work for one person may be too restrictive for another. A few years ago, I stepped in a hole and sprained my ankle severely enough that I'm now an excess pronator. The first motion-control shoe I tried was so stiff it felt as though I had bricks on my feet. Within two days, both of my knees were sore—but rather than hurting on the inside, as tends to happen with overpronation, they hurt on the outside, as happens with excess supination. The shoes had shifted me from one extreme to the other.

The same can happen to you if you overcorrect a pronation problem, particularly one that isn't causing you harm. As a beginner, of course, you have no choice but to defer to the shoe-store experts, and in your first months of start-up, you're going to be running low enough mileage that you probably won't have much problem no matter what you buy. But if, as you progress, you find that you're fighting the shoe or getting pain on either the inside or the outside of the knee, it may be time to shift shoes or invest in orthotics (see pages 83–84).

If the Shoe Fits . . .

Once you've determined what type of shoes you need—narrowing the choices, perhaps, to a couple of models—the next step is to find ones that fit properly.

The basic rule is simple: running shoes should fit snugly, but not so snugly they hurt. Otherwise, your feet slop around inside them, depriving you of the most efficient toe-off (see pages 91–92) with each stride. Overly large shoes will also throw off the position of the arch support, forefoot cushioning, and other features designed to affect the shoe's comfort and stability. If you insist on buying shoes that are too large, you will undo a lot of the expensive engineering you're paying for. Even more significantly, you will set yourself up for foot pain. A mispositioned arch support can cause your arch to cramp, and all that slipping and sliding inside an overly large shoe can give you blisters, particularly on downhills, when gravity is trying to jam your foot forward into the shoe.

So, what's the best size for a running shoe? Ideally, when you're standing with your weight fully on one foot, wearing the socks you'd use to run, your toes should be no farther than ¼ inch from the shoe's tip. How close you'll be able to come will depend on the degree to which the shape of your feet and the shoe's toe box coincide. If your toes are unusual—a particular problem for people with Morton's foot (see page 65)—you'll have to make more compromises than people whose feet more closely match the shoemaker's image.

A lot of runners, even experienced ones, buy shoes that are too big, frequently leaving a half-inch gap between their toes and the tip of the shoe. Maybe they're remembering childhood shoe shopping, when their parents tried to buy everything a couple sizes too large so that it wouldn't be immediately outgrown. But running shoes work best when they're snug. When I was training for world-class races, I'd always seek out shoes sized so my toes would just barely touch the tip. There's enough elasticity in most shoes that they would then stretch a bit when I needed it, while always being perfectly supportive. A useful analogy is buying automotive driving gloves. If the gloves are too loose, you can't get a good grip on the wheel. For the same reason, shoes should also be snug fitting.

Obviously, you should walk around in the shoe for several minutes before buying it. If that makes your foot uncomfortable, then the shoe's clearly too tight for running. Overly tight shoes will bruise toenails or give you toe blisters. If the shoe feels comfortable, test out the next size smaller, to see if it might work even better. Running shoes don't stretch with age and don't need to be broken in like leather shoes, so the shoes should fit perfectly from the moment you first try them on.

Running shoes should be laced as snugly as possible without discomfort. For longer runs or races, you'll want to jog a few blocks after putting them on, then retie them more snugly to remove unwanted slack. The best laces are flat, not round, because they're less likely to come untied. If your shoes come with round laces, particularly if they're nylon, you may want to replace them with something less likely to work loose.

Shoemakers often create fancy lacing patterns that may need to be explained by the shoe clerk. The top eyelets, for example, may be positioned well toward the back and sides of the shoe to help pull the heel counter more snugly against the heel. Some people like this, others don't. Feel free to experiment with it after you've purchased the shoe; if you don't like it, you can always skip those eyelets. If the lace is too long without using the eyelets, replace it with a shorter one, double knot the excess, or tuck the leftover length beneath the other laces where it won't immediately flop free.

Some people, particularly those who have extremely narrow feet, find they need different lace tightness for the toes and the forefoot. An easy way to achieve this is to cross the laces in a simple overhand knot (the type of over-and-under twist you put in them at the start of tying a normal shoelace bow) at the desired dividing point. With a few seconds' effort, you can now independently adjust lace tightness above and below this knot.

Narrow-footed people may also have to pull the laces extremely tight to keep their heels from slipping. If this leaves the laces binding too tightly into your forefoot, you may be able to solve the problem with a scrap of foam padding tucked beneath the laces. Thicker socks with a space-consuming heel cushion may also help. An even better solution, of course, is to find shoes made for narrow feet, but such models are relatively uncommon and may severely limit your choice of brands and models. New Balance specializes in such shoes, and Nike's shoes tend to run slightly narrower than average. Narrow-footed orthotic wearers will have less problem finding suitable shoes because the orthotic eats up a lot of room in the shoe.

Trail Shoes

Some shoes are designed more for trail running than for road running. You probably won't want a pair of these for your first running shoes, but if you do a lot of trail running, you may someday consider buying a set as a second pair. Their principal difference from road shoes is a slightly beefier build, designed to protect your foot from bruising collisions with rocks and to give added stability on uneven surfaces. They're also made with heavier materials so the shoe won't wear out quickly from scrapes against rocks or sticks. Specifically, they have a sturdier toe box and perhaps a wider and slightly more flared heel. Some people find they can serve double duty as light-duty hiking shoes.

Very few people need specialty trail shoes. You can do occasional trail running in road shoes, unless you're running in extremely rough conditions.

Conversely, you can run the roads in trail shoes, although they may feel a bit heavy and clunky. As a beginner, you should not be doing rough-duty trail running until you've gotten into basically good aerobic condition and have run long enough to build up strength in your ankles, reducing the risk of a sprain.

TEN COMMANDMENTS OF SHOE PURCHASES

1. Don't scrimp on purchasing shoes, which are your first line of defense against injuries.
2. Seek professional advice at a specialty running store.
3. Bring well-worn street shoes with you for your first purchase; bring your worn-out running shoes with you for later purchases.
4. Wear the same type of socks you'll wear running.
5. If you use orthotics, have them with you.
6. Don't be afraid to admit you're a beginner. The clerks will be happy to welcome you to their favorite sport, and they'll know you're not planning on putting in high mileage in the near future.
7. Make sure your shoes fit snugly, with no more than ¼ inch of extra room at the toes.
8. Make sure your running shoes fit properly from the start, because they don't break in.
9. Remember that shoe weight is irrelevant in training shoes.
10. Don't let high-tech designs, pretty colors, or marketing hype seduce you into buying shoes that don't feel right on your feet.

Racing Shoes

These featherlight shoes are for serious racers. They're designed for speed first, comfort second. They're also less durable than training shoes.

You needn't be a regular age-group winner to benefit from racing shoes, but there's no sense shelling out $75 for them unless you have a couple of years of racing experience and are already doing speed training (as discussed in chapter 11). At most, racing shoes will probably give you 20 to

30 extra seconds in a 10-kilometer race. If you get a pair, wear them only for racing. This not only will extend the life of the shoe, but it will help you avoid injuries from training in such lightly constructed footwear.

Shoe Wear

Running shoes are typically good for about 800 to 1,000 miles—more if you run mostly on treadmills or other nonabrasive surfaces, less if you're heavy, prefer abrasive concrete or asphalt, or run with a twisting, grinding foot motion that eats up soles. Unless you do a lot of trail running or use your shoes for muddy, rocky hiking, it's rarely the upper that wears out. The earliest and most important signs of wear are generally in the soles.

The first thing to look for is compression in the *midsole*, the thick layer of cushioned material between the hard outer sole and the inner lining beneath your foot. After enough foot strikes, any substance other than gel or air will eventually compress. This is why some running shoes have evolved ever-more-prominent gel or air pockets. Like pneumatic tires, these pockets will retain their cushion unless something punctures them. But even these shoes won't last forever. The air or gel must be held in place by foam, and that foam will gradually compress.

Typically, compression appears first beneath the outside, rear corner of the heel, where your foot strikes with the most force. This compression will gradually cause the shoe to tilt toward the outside, causing your foot to roll farther and farther that way each time it hits the ground. Much like excess supination, this movement transfers an unnatural shock up your legs, where it can cause problems anywhere from your knees to your hips.

With experience, you can spot a worn-out shoe just by looking at it. But when you're starting out, the best way to check your shoes is to have a friend watch from behind as you stand in them. First, stand barefoot or in a pair of new walking shoes for comparison. The tendency of your feet to roll

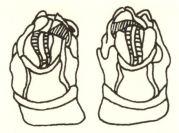

Severely worn-out running shoes.

outward in worn-out shoes will now be obvious. A little bit of compression is tolerable, but anything more than ⅛ inch means it's time for new shoes.

Even if the midsole never compresses, you're going to gradually wear away the outer sole material, again most strongly at the shoes' outside, back corners. This, too, will cause them to cant outward until eventually you need replacements. If the soles are starting to wear through to the midsoles, it's long past time to retire them from running. With the protective outer layer gone, the midsole will rapidly abrade, eventually popping any gel or air pockets. Relegate the shoes to walking, and shift your aging walking shoes to gardening, canoeing, or other throwaway uses. One side benefit of running is that it gives you a continual supply of disposable shoes.

When I was training seriously, I switched to new shoes about every 200 miles—which at the time meant about every two weeks. They wouldn't have much wear by most people's standards, but running 100 miles or more a week, I was always pushing the envelope, where any little problem can lead to injury. There was no way I'd risk any noticeable compression in their soles. Now, running only 30 miles a week for fun and fitness, I can get about eight months' use out of each pair.

> **Running shoes should fit snugly. Otherwise, your feet slop around inside them, depriving you of the most efficient toe-off with each stride.**

Shoe Maintenance

You'll get more use from each pair of shoes if you take proper care of them. To start with, if you're trying to conserve your shoe budget, there's no reason to wear $90 running shoes for casual walking. Concrete eats shoe sole material more quickly than almost any other surface does, and mile for mile, walking seems to be nearly as abrasive as running. It's also good to let your running shoes dry completely between uses—something that won't happen if you're always wearing them around the house.

Shoe Glue or similar products can be used to extend the life of shoe soles. A lot like model airplane cement, it's applied in thin layers to the bottom of the sole. The idea is that when the glue wears off, it can be replaced, protecting the shoe material itself. You can even use the glue in thicker layers to compensate for small amounts of midsole compression. The product was particularly popular in the early 1980s, when even the best outer soles could wear through to midsole in only a few hundred miles. Its downside is that it's softer than modern sole material and has to be replaced frequently. Most people today don't bother.

You can also ask a shoe repair store to resole your shoes, as long as all you're replacing is the outer sole. But by the time a shoe needs resoling, the midsole is probably too worn-out to make it worth the effort. It's like repainting a rusted-out automobile; the result may look nice, but underneath the car is still a junker.

I wash my shoes about every two weeks. I use cold water and the gentle cycle, and I don't put them in the dryer. Most shoes are made with a lot of glue that may melt and fall apart in a clothes dryer. But by avoiding hot water and the dryer, I've never had any problems washing a shoe. I've even heard that it makes them last longer.

SOCKS

First, a hint: if you're buying shoes and socks at the same time, choose the socks first, so you can wear them when fitting the shoes.

You can do your workouts in almost any type of socks, but running socks are a small investment that's worth the money. For $10 or less, you can get socks with extra cushion in the heels and forefoot, for fewer blisters and longer wear. You can also buy them in a variety of thicknesses to help fine-tune your shoe comfort for those days when your feet inexplicably swell, altering the fit of shoes that have been comfortable for hundreds of miles. Super-thin socks tend to be for weight-conscious racers only; they may rub and create "hot spots" on your feet. You'll probably be happier in thicker socks that mold to your foot and allow less chance of blister-inducing rubbing.

Running socks range from low-cut to crew length. Choose whichever you like, as long as they're tall enough not to slide down your ankle and bunch up uncomfortably in your shoe. Crew-length socks are considerably warmer, so you might want the anklet variety for hot weather, switching to something that comes farther up your calf when the weather's cool enough for you to be wearing tights.

Sock material also varies. Cotton feels extremely comfortable when you first put it on, but it absorbs moisture and holds it next to your foot for the duration of the run. This can make your socks too warm in hot weather and uncomfortably cold and damp in cool weather. It may also cause blisters. Polyester is best for wicking moisture away from the foot, and the latest polyesters such as CoolMax or Dri Fit come fairly close to the feel of cotton. Acrylic fabrics split the difference in comfort—and in wicking ability. Most people find the better polyesters to be comfortable enough to be the optimum choice.

Although socks have become nearly as high-tech as shoes, the basic rule is simpler: buy what feels comfortable and looks good to you. Even if a sock proves to be a bad choice, as a beginner you're not going to be all that far from home when you discover it. By the time you've worked up to a point where this might be a concern, you'll have learned what your feet need.

SHORTS AND SHIRTS

There was a time when specialty running togs came only as those skimpy short shorts and sleeveless singlets favored by racers. If your modesty or physique couldn't bear such exposure, your only other choice was a T-shirt and gym shorts.

For fitness running, of course, you can still dress in gym shorts and a cotton T-shirt if you want. Many runners do. But attire designed specifically for running has its advantages, and manufacturers have awakened to the fact that fitness runners, not racers, dominate the market. Now you can buy the latest space-age fabric without needing to look like you're decked out for the Olympics. High-tech shirts and shorts come in virtually any style you want, ranging from tank tops and racing shorts to long-sleeved zip-necked shirts and shorts that come nearly to your knees, like basketball shorts. There are even tops that look like old-fashioned T-shirts.

The hallmark of running apparel isn't its appearance so much as it is the fabric it's made from. Just as cotton isn't ideal for running socks, cotton T-shirts and nylon or cotton shorts hold so much sweat that they easily become heavy, dripping lumps of fabric. A better choice is the panoply of fabrics that wick moisture away from the skin so you not only feel more comfortable when running but are less apt to become chilled afterward. Brand names include Dri Fit, CoolMax, Capilene, and many others. Expect to spend about $25 to $35 for a short-sleeved shirt and $30 to $50 for a long-sleeved one. The exact price will depend on whether the shirt is summer or winter weight, and whether the neck has a zipper to control ventilation.

Good running shorts provide complete freedom of motion and are also made of a noncotton fabric that doesn't absorb enormous quantities of chafe-inducing moisture. They may also have an inner liner and a small pocket for a key or telephone change. Don't trust the key pocket with anything vital, however, unless you use a safety pin to keep it shut. Some shorts have larger zipper pockets where you can store something bigger, such as an energy bar, a credit card, or a few dollar bills. Many shorts and some tops also have reflective stripes for evening running. These cost anywhere from $20 to $35.

Women's Tops

Sports tops ($30 to $45) have revolutionized women's running apparel. Often called *sports bras*, they needn't be worn solely as undergarments. Rather, they are outer garments with built-in support.

Sport tops have improved significantly since their development in the 1970s. The latest garments provide good support without restricting breathing. Robin Roberts, Nike's manager for women's running apparel, recommends that buyers avoid tops with thin shoulder straps and scoop backs; the wider *racer back* provides greater support while allowing full arm motion. A good wicking fabric also adds to comfort. Roberts advises turning the garment inside out when shopping for a sports top to look for support-providing construction details. Examine seams with an eye to their potential for chafing.

Preventing Chafing

Worried about chafing when you run? Chafing used to afflict me even at my thinnest. My favorite solution was petroleum jelly. I've known people who, in longer races (over 10K), would even swab the stuff between their toes. Although most people shouldn't need to do that you may need to lubricate such spots as the insides of your thighs. Lycra or Spandex shorts, cut like bicycling shorts but without the padded seat cushion found on true cycling shorts, can also be an instant solution for thigh chafing. Sleeveless singlets may cause you to chafe beneath the arms, particularly in hot, humid weather.

Men may be surprised to find that their nipples chafe against the insides of their shirts. This is mostly a marathoner's problem, but it occasionally happens in just a few minutes of easy running, particularly in warm, muggy weather. The typical culprit: cotton T-shirts with heavy, stiff design patterns. The simplest solution for fitness running: find another shirt, or switch to a noncotton fabric that stays drier when you sweat.

RAIN GEAR

Rain gear is the most expensive running clothing you'll need. You can get away with your everyday running wear on a hot summer day, when getting wet feels good, but in cooler weather you'll want something water resistant.

A good jacket will cost $70 to $200, and rain pants will cost $50 to $90. Don't try substituting an inexpensive nylon jacket. A $30 jacket can be impressively waterproof, but it won't breathe. Good running jackets are made of water-resistant fabrics that don't do quite such a good job of keeping moisture from coming in but that do a far better job of letting your sweat get out. The original waterproof-breathable fabric was Gore-Tex, but by modern standards it's relatively low on the breathability scale. It's good for the lower exertion rates of hikers and fishermen, but not for runners. You need something that breathes even better—and there are a host of fabrics called *micropore fabrics* that do just this. Any well-designed running jacket will use one of these fabrics.

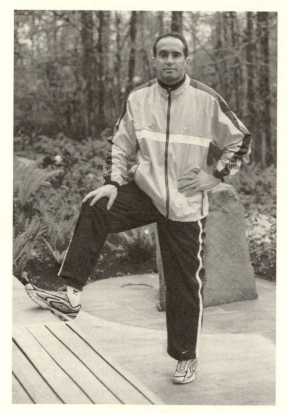

Here I'm dressed for running in cool, damp conditions.

Good running jackets also have air vents for even better air circulation. These vents may be placed beneath flaps across the back, under the arms, across the chest, or in the pockets. Some flaps may have zippers to give you control over the degree of airflow. Flaps and zippers add to the price, but if you use the jacket a lot they're worth it.

In cold climates like New England's, you're going to want a full jacket. In damp but moderate-temperature environments like in the Pacific Northwest, vests are popular. These vests cost about $45 to $80 and are typically worn over a long-sleeved shirt made of a warm-when-wet wicking fabric.

Rain pants needn't be as expensively designed because your legs don't sweat as much as your upper body. You'll probably want loose-fitting *track pants*, made of the same type of fabric as your rain jacket. Alternatively, you may just use cold-weather tights and let them get wet. Don't use stirrup tights (rare these days), because they'll conduct water down into your shoes.

HOT AND COLD RUNNING

The drawbacks of cotton are magnified by temperatures at either extreme of the comfort scale. As long as you avoid cotton, choosing your attire simply means wearing more or less of the same fabrics that work best under more moderate conditions.

In hot weather, you'll want lightweight, well-ventilated clothes that won't become clingy and heavy when you sweat. But you will also need a balance between sunburn risk and keeping cool. A baseball-style cap with a breathable mesh top and a bill to keep the sun off your face will help, but you also need to think about sunburned shoulders before you don one of those summer *singlets* (sleeveless tank tops for runners; about $18 to $30). One state-of-the-art singlet (by Nike) is made of a breathable mesh underlain by tiny knobs—like the fabric pilling that forms on old sweaters. These knobs space the mesh away from your skin for added airflow, *and* they reduce the risk of being sunburned through the mesh.

What you'll want for cold-weather running depends on just how cold it is. The basic rule is that beginners tend to overdress. As long as you're wearing something that adequately cuts the wind, it's amazing how little else you will need to wear to run at subfreezing temperatures.

Start with a long-sleeved top made of a good synthetic fabric. Avoid cotton sweatshirts. Backpackers and other wilderness aficionados have a slogan: Cotton kills. However warm cotton may feel while you're walking around the yard, when you sweat in it, it loses virtually all of its insulating ability. When running, you're not likely to be in remote areas where this might be deadly, but this characteristic of cotton will make you unhappy. Get an adequately warm top made of the same type of fabrics that work best for moderate-season use. For really cold conditions, wear your rain jacket or vest over the top. If that won't do the trick, you probably live in Minnesota, Montana, Manitoba, or some other northern clime and already know more than most runners about cold-weather attire. Even there, a microfleece jacket and pants under a rainsuit as windbreaker should do the trick.

Here I'm dressed for temperatures just below freezing.

Your legs will be adequately protected in tights, windproof track pants, or both. Some tights have outer liners of windproof fabrics.

Unfortunately for beginners, there are no hard-and-fast guidelines to what is adequate. Cold-acclimated runners might be comfortable in long-sleeved shirts and shorts at temperatures that would stop Texans or Californians in their tracks. Experimentation is the only way to find out what you'll need. Start with lightweight Lycra or Spandex tights and add another layer or buy heavier tights or track pants as temperatures dip through the fall. Above all, do not risk frostbite by running in conditions too cold for your heaviest running apparel. Buy warmer clothes or wait for the cold snap to end.

The cost of the clothing depends on the climate. For January in Vermont, you can probably buy a warm fleece top, a rain and wind jacket, and good windproof tights for about $200 to $250. In a moderate winter climate like the Pacific Northwest, you can get thinner versions of the same attire for about $140.

UNDERWEAR

Underwear choice is mostly a matter of comfort and modesty. The liners in running shorts are often designed to substitute for underwear, although men may find they don't have enough support. Whatever your high school physical education teacher may once have told you, men don't need athletic supporters to run; bikini-style briefs will do fine. Jockey shorts, however, aren't adequate and will chafe uncomfortably when soaked with sweat.

Women have more choices, both in style and in fabric. In addition to the traditional nylon and cotton, women's underwear is beginning to be made in the same moisture-wicking fabrics used for shirts and shorts. With luck, men's underwear will soon follow suit. Better fabrics would definitely help those with chafing problems.

TOYS AND GADGETS

Although running is basically a low-tech sport, innovative sports companies provide a steady stream of gadgetry for those with the time, interest, and pocketbooks to be drawn to it.

Sports watches. Because the running program outlined in chapter 2 is based on time rather than distance, you're going to need a watch. Although there are watches with built-in calculators to compute your pace, enough memory to store months of workouts, and computer jacks to download all of that information to a computer, you needn't buy anything so complex. In fact, the fancy watches may have you spending all of your time consulting the owner's manual to remember how to do simple things like turning the stopwatch function on and off.

At the other end of the spectrum, you can get by with your normal day-to-day watch, as long as it won't be ruined by sweat. Or you can buy a sports watch with a stopwatch feature for as little as $10—although $20 to $30 will get you a more reliable model that's waterproof enough even for swimming. If you take up racing, you may want a watch that can record your pace at each mile so you can later analyze your performance. But such watches are mixed blessings, particularly during the stress and excitement of a race. It's far too easy to hit the wrong button and reset the timer to zero rather than recording the desired reading in the watch's memory.

At this stage, anything more than a simple digital stopwatch is potentially counterproductive. Your goal is relatively relaxed, heartbeat-elevating running, not perpetually racing the clock from block to block. If a fancy sports watch would induce a shift toward a racing mentality, don't get it until you're ready to take up racing.

Heart rate monitors. Heart rate monitors run a band around your chest, sending a low-energy radio pulse to a specially designed wristwatch that gives an instantaneous readout of your pulse rate. (If you and a jogging partner use the same brand, you may need to keep a few feet apart to keep the signals from interfering.) At a cost of $80 to $180, heart rate monitors are far more useful for the average runner than high-tech watches are because they tend to keep you from going too fast, rather than encouraging you to race the clock.

Heart rate monitors aren't mandatory. You can always measure your pulse by counting heartbeats with a stopwatch. But that's hard to do on the move, and you're not likely to do it all that often. The monitor gives you instant feedback. It also tells you whether that sluggish feeling at the end of a run is simply a psychological barrier or a "real" effect due to muscles being pushed into unfamiliar territory. In the former case, the monitor will tell you that your pulse hasn't changed. In the latter case, you'll find that it is increasing, giving you permission to slow down. As emphasized in chapter 2, whether you're running purely for fitness or with an eye to someday becoming involved in racing, speed isn't what matters. What's important at this stage is attaining a modestly (but not overly) elevated heart rate and training your body to maintain this rate over the course of your run.

Some heart rate monitors have beepers that inform you if your pulse strays out of the desired range. It's a personal choice, but many people find these beepers irritating, and you may not be welcome if you wear one with a group of other runners. As a practical matter, beepers also aren't particularly necessary. Suppose you've set the beeper to sound if your heart rate strays out of the range between 120 and 130 beats a minute. If your normal running pace produces a heart rate of 125 beats a minute, it's going to take a fairly substantial change in effort to move you outside this range—not something you're likely to overlook if you occasionally check the readout.

Pedometers. These are gadgets that attach to your waist or lace into your shoes to measure distance by counting paces. They're inexpensive but not terribly accurate, partly because your stride length will vary depending on whether you're going uphill or down or whether the wind is in your face or at your back. Your stride length will also change as you gain running experience and gradually speed up. This means that pedometers need to be recalibrated occasionally. The most accurate way to calibrate a pedometer is to find a quarter-mile or 400-meter track and count the number of paces it takes to circle it once.

If you like toys, there's no reason not to get a pedometer, but you'll probably get a more accurate measure of distance by knowing your average pace (check it occasionally on a measured route) and comparing that to your stopwatch readings.

Key wallets and fanny packs. If you're lucky enough to be able to run from your home or office, you may not need to carry anything with you. But sometimes it's fun to drive somewhere more distant for a pleasant running route or to meet a group of other runners. Or maybe you live alone and have to take at least a door key with you when you're out running.

There are three basic ways to carry keys and other small items. If the key is small enough, you may be able to attach it to your shorts with a safety pin or carry it in the shorts' tiny coin pocket. Another alternative is a *shoe wallet*, which attaches to your shoelaces. Shoe wallets are large enough to hold your keys, a few dollar bills, and maybe a driver's license, bus pass, medical alert card, or credit cards, allowing you to leave your main wallet safely at home while still being adequately equipped for driving or having a postrun lunch with friends.

A third alternative is a fanny pack. The easiest packs to use are barely larger than your billfold and have separate, easily accessible pockets for keys and a wallet. Large fanny packs designed for hikers will probably bounce uncomfortably when you run. Get a larger pack if you need to carry a cell phone, asthma inhaler, bee-sting kit, or pepper spray. You can get either a key wallet or a wallet-sized fanny pack for as little as $15. Be aware that anything in a fanny pack is apt to get sweaty, and shoe wallets will get wet from puddles.

Water-bottle carriers. Conventional fanny packs for runners are designed for wallets and keys and not much else. If you also want a water bottle, you will need a special fanny pack that holds the bottle upright in a mesh pocket where you can reach it on the run. These packs allow you to position the water bottle wherever you want it around your waist, but most likely you'll want to place it at the small of your back. Pull the belt buckle tight enough to keep the pack from bouncing around, without snugging it so firmly that it interferes with your breathing.

Carrying water with you on the run generally isn't necessary unless the weather is very, very hot or you're going to be out for more than 30 minutes. Even then, many runners prefer to pick routes with water fountains that offer convenient excuses for rest breaks. If you do carry water, don't forget to drink it; take a good swig about every 10 minutes.

Sweatbands. Sweatbands keep sweat—and rain—out of your eyes. Some people love them; some don't. They're inexpensive enough that it's easy to experiment. You can also get sweatbands for your wrists and ankles, although these are more popular in aerobics classes than they are for running.

Personal stereos. Many people can't imagine running without taking their music along with them. Personal stereos, however, are best restricted to treadmill running. When used outdoors, they mask traffic sounds and induce daydreaming, increasing your risk of collision with cars, bicycles, or other runners. By distracting you from the running process, they also encourage you to view running as something that must be endured, rather than a potentially joyous pursuit in its own right. If you phase into running gradually enough and seek out pleasant places to run, you may find that you'd much rather live in the "now" of the run itself, rather than hiding from it in a world of music or talk radio. Minimizing personal stereo usage will also keep you more aware of what's going on with your body, moment to moment—a particularly useful skill if you may someday take up racing.

Ankle weights and hand weights. A few years ago, it was a fad for joggers to strap weights to their ankles to increase the effort required to run. The theory was that the extra effort would get you in shape more quickly. In reality, this is an extremely bad idea because it alters the biomechanics of your stride. Great marathoners can run 120 miles a week because their legs are as close to biomechanically perfect as anyone's on earth. Most runners aren't blessed with such perfect strides, and there will be some level at which their bodies will break down under the strain. Strapping weights to your ankles simply reduces this injury threshold, making you more likely to encounter it at fitness-running levels. If this fad ever returns, resist it as the foolishness it is.

Hand weights are a little different. They're often used by power walkers, who are trying to build upper-body strength as they walk. Some runners have tried them, but they're not popular, probably because running with even 1-pound weights in your hands simply isn't much fun. It's also not of any cardiovascular benefit. Treadmill studies have shown that carrying hand weights slows down your running pace enough that you get no more exercise with them than without. Hand weights probably won't get you injured, but you can get the same upper-body benefits, while having more fun running, with the weightlifting routine described in chapter 7.

ORTHOTICS

Orthotics are shoe inserts designed to compensate for abnormalities in your feet. Mass-produced arch supports may be labeled as orthotics, but true orthotics are custom-made, come in a variety of construction materials and

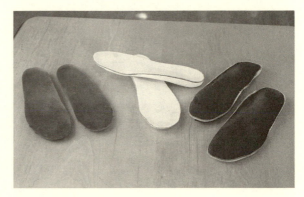

Three full-length orthotics styles.

styles, and cost upward of $150. They're durable, although changes in your feet may require them to be replaced about every three years.

You can obtain orthotics by prescription from your doctor, but a prescription isn't necessary unless it's required by your health insurance company. Getting an insurance company to pay for an orthotic, however, is often more trouble than it's worth. You'll probably need to wait until you're injured, then find a sympathetic doctor who's interested in preventing a recurrence of the injury rather than just telling you to lay off from running while it heals. Even then, many insurance policies specifically exclude orthotics.

If you decide to buy an orthotic on your own, skip the doctor and go straight to the specialists who make them. Ask for referrals from other runners, a running store, or a chiropractor interested in sports medicine. Or check the Yellow Pages for makers of "orthopedic appliances," seeking a certified pedorthist, if available. Podiatrists can also refer you to the proper people.

Orthotics aren't just for foot pain. By correcting your foot motion, you can also eliminate problems in the Achilles tendons, knees, and hips. The classic sign that you may need orthotics is if your body repeatedly breaks down whenever you hit a particular level of training, regardless of how slowly you progress. That typically means something's wrong with your stride, and your feet are the most likely culprit.

You may also need orthotics if

- you have excess pronation that is not sufficiently corrected by motion-control shoes
- you have Morton's foot
- you've ever broken your ankle (the bones may not have set quite correctly)
- you have a history of ankle sprains (the orthotic will help stabilize your foot and reduce its tendency to twist)
- you have degenerative arthritis in your knees (orthotics can alter the stress points so you can be active without pain)

A Note on Orthotics

If you normally wear any type of arch support, heel lift, or orthotic device, make sure you tell the clerk and bring it with you when shoe shopping. These devices substitute for the foam insole that comes with the shoe (except for heel lifts, which can slide under the foam) and can radically change the shoe's fit. If you wear such devices, you're probably wasting your money if you buy shoes without first testing how they fit with the orthotic.

Running store clerks will know which styles of shoes work best with orthotics. The biggest concern is to avoid putting a full-length orthotic (any device that stretches forward from the heel to beyond the ball of the foot) in a curve-lasted shoe unless the orthotic was designed for use in such shoes. Otherwise, the midpoint of the orthotic will hang over to the side of the curved shoe, squashing down every time you put weight on it. This may not be good for a $200 orthotic, and it may also help wear out the shoe more quickly. But more importantly, it means the orthotic will be less able to stop your foot from rolling inward with each stride, as it was probably intended to do. In short, putting a straight orthotic in a curve-lasted shoe will deprive you of part of the orthotic's function—a major consideration for orthotic wearers, since most U.S. running shoes are curve lasted. The bottom line is simple: make sure your orthotist knows what type of shoes you intend to wear them in before you plunk down the bucks for orthotics.

5

RUNNING FORM

CHILDREN INSTINCTIVELY KNOW HOW TO RUN. They do it with simple abandon, often with nearly flawless form. But as we age, most of us lose that ability. Perhaps it's from reduced flexibility, or perhaps we accumulate bad habits by forcing ourselves, for whatever reason, to move unnaturally.

The best time to curb these habits is when you're beginning. It's not impossible to do so later, but the more miles you've logged without correcting errors in your stride, the more firmly entrenched the habits become. Furthermore, the gradual, gentle-on-the-joints start-up program outlined in chapter 2 offers an ideal opportunity to perfect your form because it's much easier to concentrate on form if you're only running a few minutes at a time. If you start pushing yourself to longer distances before correcting your stride, you'll revert to bad habits the moment you get tired. Starting slowly is important, therefore, even if your ultimate goal is high-mileage race training. The earlier you start learning good form, the fewer bad habits you'll develop.

Even if running quickly and efficiently isn't your goal, a good stride is valuable. Learning to run correctly reduces the risk of injuries and makes your workouts easier, more natural, and a lot more fun. When people talk of the runner's high, part of it is simply the joy that comes from moving fluidly, with no wasted effort. Pay attention to your stride when you're beginning, and you'll have many more of those magic moments later on.

UPPER-BODY FORM

Proper stride is a mix of upper-body and lower-body motions. The two are connected: errors in the upper body translate to inefficient leg motion.

The most obvious aspect of upper-body motion is your arm swing. Beginning runners tend to make one of two mistakes: either they hold their arms limply down near their hips, or they wag them in an unnatural sideways motion with each swing.

Pause for a moment to consider the mechanics of running. Your arms and legs move in cross-body tandem. For example, as your right arm swings forward, your left leg draws forward and upward, ready for the next foot plant. You've known this since you learned to walk. If the arm and leg

Proper arm swing brings your hand near the centerline of your body, at about nipple height.

swing weren't properly synchronized, you'd stagger around with each stride, trying not to fall over sideways. But just as the timing of the arm swing maintains your balance, the degree of swing governs important aspects of your foot motion. If you hold your hands nearly immobile down near your hips, you'll be forced into tiny, choppy strides—inefficient, slow, and not very comfortable. If you pump them all the way up to shoulder height, you'll be able to lift your knees into an exaggerated high step—also inefficient and energy wasting.

Obviously, what you want is something in the middle. The optimum arm swing brings your hands up to about the level of your nipples. If you have access to a treadmill, set up a mirror and watch yourself for a while; otherwise, recruit a friend to help you find the proper motion. Even on your own, you ought to be able to tell within a couple of inches where your hands are at the peak of their trajectory. Then, it's just a matter of practice.

Your arm swing also has a sideways component. Many beginners wave their arms out to the side with each forward swing, in an exaggerated motion as though they're trying to waltz with a bear. That forces your legs to waddle inefficiently from side to side. Instead, you want your feet to move as straight ahead with each stride as possible, so that each step is carrying you toward your goal rather than bouncing even slightly back and forth. If you find yourself doing this outward-swinging arm motion, now is the time to curb it.

In theory, you'd run your fastest if your arms drove forward and back in exactly the direction you're moving. That, in fact, is exactly how the best sprinters run. But it's tiring, and you can't keep it up for long. In distance running, your arms should swing inward as they come forward, with your hands coming approximately to your breastbone. If they swing substantially farther than midway across your body, you'll find yourself moving down the road with an odd, energy-wasting hip twist as your body overrotates with each stride. Slightly too little inward motion is less of a problem, but you'll move more smoothly if you can get that arm swing to terminate naturally at your breastbone, at approximately nipple height.

You'll also benefit from controlling the lean of your upper body. Many beginners lean backward. Others have been told to lean forward. Both positions are wrong. Your natural running motion has the torso close to verti-

Many beginners lean too far back (left) or too far forward (right).

cal, or leaning only slightly forward, at most. Leaning forward is the way to run quickly downhill (see pages 95–96). If you do it on the flats, in essence you'll be trying to plant your feet slightly below road surface with each stride. That's impossible, of course, so instead you land uncomfortably, with an inefficient, shorter-than-normal stride.

If you lean backward, you have an even worse problem. Now, your feet are trying to land in midair. Obviously, this won't happen, so they'll continue swinging forward before hitting the pavement, too far out in front of you and too far back on your heels—a motion known as *reaching out*. We discuss this problem in the Leg Motion section below; for now, remember that leaning backward exaggerates reaching out.

Your natural running motion has the torso close to vertical, or leaning only slightly forward.

Fight the Clench

A minor but easy-to-cure form error is to ball your hands into tight fists or tense up the muscles of your upper arms and shoulders—both of which are particularly easy to do at the end of a long run. You may also find yourself clenching your jaw or tightening the muscles of your neck and shoulders. Check periodically to see if you're doing this, making this self-check an automatic part of running. Muscle clenching isn't going to ruin your stride, but it wastes energy that's better devoted to running and can leave the affected muscles feeling unnecessarily tired and "beat up" afterward. Pay particular attention to your hands; they should be in a relaxed, neutral curl, not balled into fists.

Sometimes, you will need to carry a key when you run, a task that requires keeping a sufficiently firm grip on the key to avoid accidentally throwing it in the gutter. Possible solutions are to invest in a shoe wallet (see page 81) or to attach the key to your shorts with a safety pin. But you can also put the key on a key ring large enough to slip over your index finger. This way you won't lose it even with your hand in a loose, relaxed grip.

LEG MOTION

Now let's turn to the lower body. Here, there are three principal stride abnormalities, one correctable with practice, another with orthotics, and another that may simply be a biomechanical cap on your native speed.

The major, correctable lower-body error is a problem that coaches call *overstriding*, but that might better be called *reaching out*. This occurs when your leg swings too far forward with each stride. Your foot comes down in front of your body, generally far back on the heel, where the shock of impact "puts on the brakes" with each stride—an inefficient and potentially injurious practice. Also, reaching out in that manner forces you to use your hamstring to pull yourself forward at the start of each stride, rather than immediately pushing off with the far stronger quadriceps muscles. Overstriders are "pullers," while people with normal strides are "pushers."

Reaching out is an extremely common error. In part, it comes from an attempt to speed up by lengthening your stride. But the type of stride lengthening that will indeed speed you up comes not from reaching out but from a rearward extension at the end of each pace that increases the time you spend airborne. This is why *overstriding* is a misleading term. Reaching out may feel like the obvious way to lengthen your stride, but it actually shortens it by forcing you to work inefficiently at the start of each stride, when your feet are too far forward.

Ideally, your foot should strike so that it's directly beneath your hips at the time

Good form makes even a casual jog more fun.

your weight first comes fully on it (i.e., when your shoe is fully on the ground), moving straight down at the moment it hits the pavement. But it's OK for your foot to land a few inches forward from this, as is comfortable for most people. A good distance-running stride also lands with the foot slightly back on the heel. A few people will land naturally on their toes; this isn't generally the best form, but it's probably not correctable without undue risk of injury. Don't, however, *try* to land on your toes, as a few beginners do. Most runners land naturally slightly back on their heels. Racers will be more likely to land on their toes, but only when they're pushing for speed, at paces well beyond the reach of most beginners.

Rather than worrying too much about what part of your foot hits first, concentrate on getting it to land directly beneath your hips. Glance down occasionally to see where your feet are landing. If they're striking far out in front of your body, it should be obvious. Smaller errors are harder to spot, but with practice, you'll learn to notice the alignment of your hip and foot at the moment of impact. If you decide you're overstriding, make a deliberate effort not to do so, even if it feels as if you're mincing your stride by

STRIDE REPORT

Rick has been working on his own to attempt stride improvements.

"I'd always thought I had a good stride, certainly better than that of many runners I'd watched over the years. But after working with Alberto, I became convinced that I didn't swing my arms quite high enough and that I was slightly reaching out.

"The arm swing was easy to correct, although it took constant attention not to lapse into the old habit. To work on overstriding, I got on a treadmill and ran at a steady pace, alternating between the stride I'd used for two decades, and one that felt slightly shorter—'minced,' in Alberto's terminology. I immediately felt the difference because the new stride brought my foot down more vertically, still landing slightly heel first but much flatter than before. I also felt less stress in my Achilles tendons. Out of curiosity, I began counting paces, discovering that the new stride increased my cadence from 167 paces a minute to 175—an increase of 5 percent. And the new motion feels completely natural.

"I have yet to determine how much faster this makes me—like Alberto's high-school athlete, I *feel* as though my stride is shorter—but in races and club workouts, I'm running up on people who used to fade off into the distance."

taking little, tiny steps. Remember that once you get the knack of landing each foot properly, the increased efficiency will actually speed you up significantly. As an added benefit, the proper stride will also reduce the shock of impact on your knees.

How It Works

Running speed is a mixture of two factors: stride length and the number of strides you take per minute. Reaching out often comes from trying to force a longer stride, rather than concentrating on the foot plant and toe-off and letting stride length develop naturally. Correcting that habit may initially reduce your stride length, but the increased leg speed may more than make up for it. As you develop a more powerful toe-off, you'll get a double bonus as you begin to extend your stride farther and farther behind you, the way you're supposed to run.

I once coached a talented high school runner who had a problem with reaching out. One day on the track, after he'd done a series of 220-yard sprints at a respectable 30-second pace, I got tough. "You're still overstriding," I told him. "I don't care what time you run, but I want the next 220 to be different. What I don't want is to see you overstriding on another of those 30-second repeats."

This time, his form was better. "What do you think the time was?" I asked.

He shrugged. "Thirty-one seconds? Thirty-two?"

I showed him the watch: 28 seconds. He'd sped up 6 percent while running what felt like an easier pace. That's how much overstriding hurts you, not only in terms of speed but in terms of jarring, as your body accelerates and brakes with each step.

Toe-Off

Your toes are as important to efficient running as are your legs. As you leave the ground with each stride, you rise up on your toes, stiffening them to provide a firm platform from which to launch yourself forward.

Much of this occurs unconsciously, but it's good to think about it occasionally. Ideally, the toe-off will come evenly from your first three toes. But if it comes from anywhere else—such as the little toes or the inside edge of the big toe—you're launching yourself sideways, in another of those energy-wasting zigzags we discussed earlier on page 87.

Toe-off is largely controlled by your foot structure and your shoes. Some motion-control shoes cant the forefoot outward too much for some runners, forcing the toe-off onto the little toes. This is not a problem you can easily correct by conscious effort; basically you're fighting a shoe that gives you too much motion control (see page 67). If you start feeling the pangs of plantar fasciitis (see pages 144–145) or pain on the outside of the lower leg (indicating transmission of unusual stresses upward from the foot) replace the shoe immediately. Otherwise, you may be able to use it at least occasionally until it wears out. Toeing off from the inside of the big toe is a sign of excess pronation and requires either orthotics or shoes with greater motion control.

> **Your toes are as important to efficient running as your legs are.**

Foot Alignment

Technically speaking, excess pronation and excess supination are also errors in running form, but it's almost impossible to train yourself to correct them. A better solution is to invest in the right shoes, orthotics, or both.

Another stride problem that's likely to have biomechanical roots can be observed by running through a puddle or across a patch of firm sand. Go back and examine your footprints. They should fall in a fairly straight line, with your left footprint and the right footprint no more than a few inches off center. If you were to run down the white stripe at the side of a football or soccer field, you should be able to run comfortably with both feet consistently hitting the line, rather than straddling back and forth from one side to the other. In addition, the inside edges of your footprints should point pretty close to straight ahead. If you tend to run duck-toed (toes pointing outward) or pigeon-toed (toes pointing inward), you have a potential problem. Worse is if one foot angles inward or outward more sharply than the other. Any of these patterns may indicate that something's not quite right in your legs, probably in your hips.

Observant friends may point this alignment pattern out and encourage you to correct it. It's yet another of those things that slow you down by making you toe off sideways with each stride. But the solution may not be easy. With conscious effort, you may be able to force your feet to line up in the ideal straight-ahead orientation, but your body has a reason for running this way, and forcing it to do something unnatural will probably get you hurt. Most likely, you'll just have to live with it. But first, check out your arm swing, as described above; if you're lucky, that's the cause. You can also turn to chapter 6 and concentrate on buttocks stretches. Your problem may be exacerbated by lack of flexibility.

Women with wide hips may have a similar problem with a less than ideally efficient alignment of their thighs. If you have wide hips, the natural flare of your pelvic bones will rotate your thighs so that your knees move inward with each stride. Although many women equate "hips" with "weight," it really doesn't matter what you weigh; the issue is your bone structure. Again, your body wants to zigzag as it runs. The lower leg compensates by flipping the foot out to the side, but the foot strike still comes at an angle that causes the arch to collapse inward, as in overpronation.

The only real solution for this problem is to correct the overpronation with motion-control shoes or orthotics. This is why you don't see many elite women distance runners with wide hips; more often the best of them have hips like teenage boys. But if you have a more feminine build, don't despair—a few women with your body type have made it to the top. They may have slightly awkward-looking gaits, but they've won Olympic gold. Millions of others run happily for health and fitness.

One Ideal Form

Beginners aren't the only runners who can benefit from paying attention to form. Elite athletes need to do so as well. I was a puller myself—a problem I didn't fully understand until my best racing days were past. Other racers actually tried to imitate me, assuming that if I could win marathons with that overextended, reaching-ahead gait, then it must be the best way to move. Actually, successful as I was, I would have run even better if my stride had been closer to optimal. And when I did correct it, in my mid-30s, running felt more natural than ever. And other than a mishap from stepping in a hole, I never had another injury.

I firmly believe there is only one ideal running form, that our bodies are all made to the same basic design, which functions best when used the way it's made to work. That doesn't mean good runners don't have their

PRACTICING THE BAD TO LEARN THE GOOD

Rick has a good exercise for understanding the differences in running form. Try the following.

"A great way to increase your understanding of the principles of good running form is to run a few yards with wildly wrong form. Try running with your torso leaning as far backward as possible. You'll find that you're reaching your legs far out in front of you and landing far back on your heels. When I tried this, my shins hurt, too; if I did it all the time, I'd be sure to get shin splints. Now reverse what you're doing and lean as far forward as possible without falling on your nose. You'll immediately find out what's wrong with this, too.

"You can use similar drills to highlight the reasons for proper arm swing. Try running with your thumbs hooked into your waistband so you can't swing them at all. Awkward, isn't it? Now try swinging them way out to the side, much too far across your body, or far out in front of you at eye level. You'll immediately see why these motions, too, aren't exactly optimal.

"Most of us, of course, don't have such radical stride abnormalities. But testing out these severe errors in running form can help convince you that smaller errors may have similar effects, even if they're less obvious."

idiosyncrasies; it just means that these idiosyncrasies detract, however slightly, from optimum pace.

Perhaps the greatest distance runner of all time is Haile Gebresailesse, from Ethiopia. Watching him in slow motion is an eye-opening experience. He runs with his hips thrust so far forward that they're practically leading the rest of his body. His feet come straight down at the end of each stride, with almost no braking impact, and his extension at the end of each stride is superb. Yet even he has a slight idiosyncrasy: his right arm swings too far inward with each stride. This might actually help him round the corners on a track, but is isn't the reason he developed the habit. It comes from childhood, when he used to run to school 5 miles every day. That was the arm in which he carried his books. It's a habit he's never quite shaken.

The lessons for beginners? First, good form pays off. But even the best runners have quirks. While these may cause them to deviate a bit from ideal, it's not enough to keep them from winning races. So, strive to improve your stride, but realize that nobody ever quite reaches perfection. This is just one of those challenges that keep life interesting.

UPHILL AND DOWN

Running uphill doesn't require working all that much harder than on the flats. Just slow down to maintain the same effort level or heart rate that you were doing beforehand. You should also shorten your stride so that you're not straining too hard on each toe-off, but this will probably feel natural enough that you won't have to think about it. You may also find yourself landing less strongly on your heel than normal or even on the ball of your foot. These are natural responses to going uphill.

Running downhill is trickier. Most runners tend to "put on the brakes" by deliberately overstriding and using their quadriceps muscles to hold themselves back. This is tiring and is jarring on the knees. If the slope isn't too extreme, try leaning into it a bit, increasing your leg speed (the number of steps you make per minute) to keep from falling on your face. Be particularly careful about not reaching out. Rick has a friend who kept getting sore knees from overstriding on long downhills. When she learned the cause and shortened her stride, the pain disappeared like magic.

On a steep enough slope, you're going to have to put on the brakes, but gentle slopes are a great opportunity to blast out faster than normal, just for

I'm #811 in the 1979 NCAA cross-country championships.

the sheer joy of the speed. Do keep your speed under control, however, so that you're not at risk of tripping, and switch back to a more conservative running style if you find yourself repeatedly hitting with a too-jarring impact.

RUNNING FORM CHECKLIST

To summarize, optimum running form includes the following:

- hands swinging to nipple height
- arm swing angling inward, terminating near the breastbone
- hands, arms, neck, and shoulders relaxed
- torso upright or leaning very slightly forward
- foot plant directly beneath the hip, with the foot coming down nearly vertically when it hits the ground

Some peculiarities in running form relate to idiosyncrasies of body structure. Trying to change them by force of will is very likely to get you injured. If you do any of the following, either live with them or consult an orthotist:

- landing naturally on your toes
- running with your feet angled outward or inward, despite proper arm motion
- excessively pronating or supinating

STRETCHING

6

STRONG MUSCLES LOOK GOOD because they're taut and firm, without unsightly droops or sags. But there is a potential loss of flexibility inherent in the very process of strengthening muscles. Some sports are more muscle tightening than others; running tightens muscles enough to produce lots of jokes about "inflexible runners."

The solution is stretching. As a full-time athlete, stretching was simply part of my job. When I was running at my best, I stretched for 10 to 15 minutes before and after my morning runs and again before and after my afternoon runs—a total of nearly an hour a day. Now, I stretch for only 10 to 15 minutes after each run, and if it's a day when I'm also doing another activity such as bicycling, I'll stretch only once. After years of conscientious stretching, this modest amount comes so naturally that I have no difficulty remembering to do it.

Regular stretching is critical to injury-free running because limber muscles exert less tension on tendons and ligaments. They're also less prone to muscle pulls, for the simple reason that they're better able to withstand the shock of modest overextension. Stretching also enhances performance. Tight muscles have restricted ranges of motion, constraining your stride length. Even if that robs you of only a small-sounding amount of power— say 5 percent—that's roughly equivalent to the difference between running 9½- and 10-minute miles. This difference may not matter much to fitness runners, but in racing, it's an enormous difference. And who *wants* to run slowly and inefficiently?

A huge disconnect exists, however, between most books' stretching advice and real-world practice. This is partly because our harried lifestyles make us view stretching as wasted time. But it's also because conventional advice is geared more toward performance-oriented athletes than toward the average runner. Unless you're worried about eking out a few extra seconds on a 10-kilometer road race, you don't need to spend large amounts of time stretching. Studies have shown that you get nearly as much benefit from stretching routines as short as five or six minutes. For most runners, that's enough—and like so many of the things we've discussed in this book, it's a lot better to get close to the maximum benefit with modest effort than to get no benefit from an overambitious program you're unable to follow.

Stretching needn't be done before running, although it's a good habit to limber up a bit at the outset, particularly if you know that certain muscles, such as your calves, tend to be tight. You'll get the biggest bang for your

STRETCH, DUMMY

Rick admits that stretching is something he sometimes has to force himself to do, a situation that may sound familiar to you. Here's what he has to say.

"You don't need a book to tell you the value of stretching. Your body already knows it instinctively, the same way a cat or dog instinctively stretches after a nap. That's why a gentle stretch feels so good.

"Given a chance, your body will do the same thing. If you awaken naturally in the morning, without the artificial jangle of an alarm clock, you may notice that the first thing you do, when still half-asleep, is stiffen and relax your legs and arms, much like the cat arches its back. Despite this instinctive knowledge, I, like many fitness runners, find it remarkably easy to forget to do my running stretches—or simply to procrastinate indefinitely.

"I wish I could outline a never-fail prescription for preventing this behavior, but all I have are suggestions. Tape a note to your door that reads 'S-t-r-e-t-c-h, dummy.' Choose running companions who aren't in too much of a hurry to stretch. Stretch at bus stops, while cooking dinner, even while standing on a corner waiting for the light to change. Make a habit of being early when meeting training partners so you have ample time to stretch while waiting, or plan a few minutes of free time after the run for an even-more-beneficial stretching routine—as long as you remember to do it."

buck, however, if you do the bulk of your stretching immediately after your run. If two otherwise identical runners were to do the same stretching routines, one before running and the other afterward, after six months, the one who stretched afterward would be considerably more limber.

If time is a constraint, however, you can generally do most of your stretching later in the day. Many runners with office jobs squeeze in their stretching in their offices during brief rest breaks from work. Some people even stretch while talking on the phone.

> **If two otherwise identical runners were to do the same stretching routines, one before running and the other afterward, after six months the one who stretched afterward would be considerably more limber.**

STRETCHING BASICS

Proper stretches are static or isometric. *Static stretching* means stretching slowly until you feel a pleasant pull (not pain) in the muscle. Hold that position for a few seconds, trying to relax the muscle, then cautiously extend the stretch farther, always being prepared to back off. *Isometric stretching* is similar except that between cautious extensions of the stretch, you gently contract the stretched muscle (without allowing the stretched limb to flex) rather than relaxing it. Then you relax the muscle to gently extend the stretch, as in static stretching. A recent revolution in sports training, isometric stretching is counterintuitive, but it allows you to get an even better stretch than you do with static stretching.

One of the surprises to come out of recent research is the discovery that there's no need to hold a stretch for more than a few seconds, and there's virtually no benefit from repeating the same stretch more than once. Runners were once told to do each stretch two or three times, spending at least 30 seconds for each repetition. Now we know you can do it once and that you get most of the benefit from holding it for as little as 10 seconds. This allows you to do a lot of different stretches in a few minutes.

Don't bounce when stretching. A sudden stretch makes the muscle think it's about to be hyperextended, and the muscle protects itself by reflexively contracting. The bouncing toe touches and other calisthenic stretches many of us were taught as children merely fight that reflexive contraction. They can also pull a muscle. Focus instead on stretching gently.

FIVE-MINUTE STRETCHING

Stretching should focus not only on the major muscles you use for running, such as the quadriceps, hamstrings, and calves, but also on the minor muscles of the hip and groin. Some version of the following stretches should form the core of your routine.

Lower-Body Stretches

Running uses mostly muscles below your waist, and, not surprisingly, these should be the primary focus of your stretching regimen.

Leaning calf stretch with trailing leg straight.

Calf stretch. Sometimes, the calf stretch is inaccurately referred to as the Achilles tendon stretch. Although its principal purpose is to reduce stresses on the tendon, you are actually stretching the calf muscles, not the tendon. Stand in front of a wall and lean forward, palms on the wall. (You can also brace yourself with a convenient table, desk, or railing.) One leg (the one to be stretched) will be farther from the wall than the other; how far will depend on the flexibility of your calves and the amount of heel lift in your shoes.

Keep the trailing foot flat on the floor, without rising up on your toes. Shifting most of your weight to the forward leg, dip that knee until you feel a good stretch in the trailing

Leaning calf stretch with knee of trailing leg bent slightly.

calf. Do this with the stretched leg straight; then bend it a bit at the knee, feeling how that shifts the point of the stretch downward along your calf. As long as you're on a good, nonslip surface, you can save time by stretching both calves at once.

Another stretch that achieves similar results is to mimic standing on a steep hill by propping up your toe on a block of wood, a low curb, or another elevated object. Your heel should be on the ground, calf relaxed. To increase the stretch, shift the foot forward so that the toes are propped up more steeply.

In both of these stretches, it's important to keep the foot pointing straight ahead, rather than pointed out to the sides in a V shape. Otherwise, you reduce the pull on the calf, negating much of the benefit of the stretch.

Hamstring stretch. There are several ways to do this stretch. The simplest is the standard toe touch you learned in grade school. If you can't reach your toes, just bend over and reach as far down as you comfortably can, keeping your knees straight. Really flexible people with long backs can put their palms on the floor, but these are usually dancers who've prac-

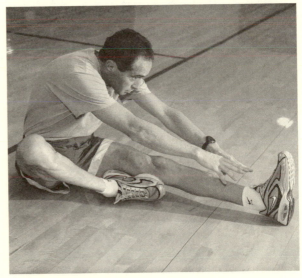

Seated hamstring stretch.

ticed for years. If you have a bad back, you may want to avoid the bent-over position of toe-touches or at least let your knees bend a bit as you stand back up.

An alternative hamstring stretch is to sit on a flat surface with one leg extended, the other comfortably out of the way. Don't sit on your heel; that's hard on the knee. Without locking the knee, lean toward the extended leg, feeling the stretch in the hamstring.

Quadriceps stretch. Many runners stretch their quads by sitting on their heels and leaning backward. A variant of this stretch is to stand on one foot, pulling the other toe upward toward your buttocks. These are indeed the most effective stretches for the quadriceps, but they should be viewed as no-nos because they also stress the front of the knee. You may be able to get away with them (I can), but you don't need that much flexibility unless you're a serious competitor or a ballet dancer.

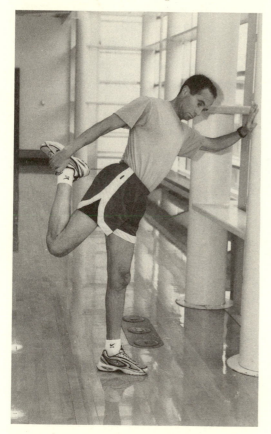

MODIFIED QUADRICEPS STRETCH.

An alternative is the *modified quadriceps stretch*. Stand on one foot, holding the other in your hand, anywhere between the toe and the ankle. If your balance is unsteady, use your free hand to brace yourself against a wall or railing. Now, without pulling your foot up toward your buttocks, press your hip forward and draw the foot horizontally backward until you feel a good stretch not only in the quadriceps but also along the front of the hip, an area that isn't stretched by the conventional quadriceps stretch.

Groin stretch. Simple but frequently overlooked, this stretch is one of an equally overlooked series that is most conveniently done in the order presented here.

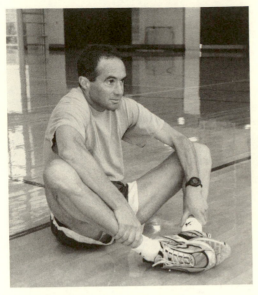

Sit on the floor, with your knees spread wide and your feet out in front of you, soles together. Viewed from above, your legs will be in the shape of a diamond. Put your elbows on your knees, placing your hands on your shins or ankles—anywhere convenient. Using your elbows, press your knees down and sideways until you feel a good stretch in the groin. It's OK to lean forward and place your chin on your clasped hands if that helps you get a better and more controlled stretch.

Groin stretch.

Figure four. This stretch is a bit complex to describe, but it's good for the hip when you get it right. Still sitting on the floor, extend one leg comfortably in front of you. Draw the other closer to you, so the knee rises above the floor, then lift the foot and put it flat on the floor on the far side of the knee of the straight leg. Maintain your balance by splaying out a hand to the side behind you.

Figure four stretch.

Let's say the left knee is the one that's extended horizontally while the right leg is the one that's drawn upright. Reach your left arm past the right side of your right knee so that the back of your arm, somewhere near the elbow, is pressed against the knee's outside. It's an odd-feeling but not uncomfortable position.

Now it's time to stretch. Rotate your torso clockwise to look backward over your right shoulder, while pressing counterclockwise with your left elbow against the knee. You should feel the stretch on the outside of your right hip. As with all of these one-leg-at-a-time stretches, reverse sides and stretch the other leg equally.

Buttocks stretches. Unwind from the figure four and lie on your back, legs extended comfortably in front of you for a final batch of three related stretches. Bend one leg about 90 degrees at the knee, and rotate it at

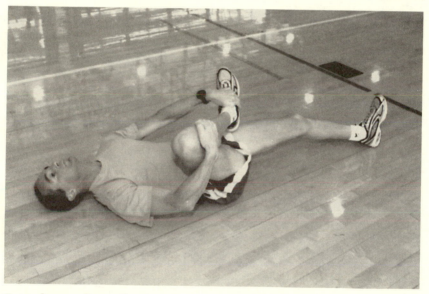

Buttocks stretch number one.

the hip so the shin is raised off the floor, roughly crossways to your body. This will bring the knee and ankle close enough to you that you should be able to reach them easily. Grasp one in each hand and pull with equal force to draw the entire lower leg toward your head. *Do not* twist the knee; rather, use both hands to move the lower leg as a unit. That's buttocks stretch number one.

Stretch number two is similar and is easy to get into from this position.

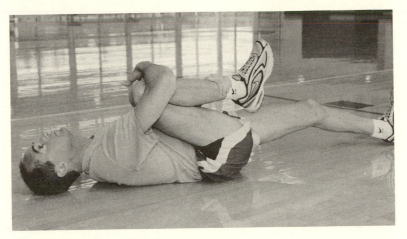

Buttocks stretch number two.

Release your grip on the ankle and, keeping the leg raised off the ground, knee bent, rotate it so the shin now lines up with your body. Clasp your hands around the knee, anywhere convenient between the kneecap and the top of the shin. Again, pull the knee toward your nose, stretching a slightly different part of the buttocks.

Finally, for buttocks stretch number three, raise the leg high above the ground, but with the knee still somewhat toward your stomach. If you can reach that far, clasp your hands behind the ankle and pull, again more or less toward your nose. You can also do this with the leg straight, for a hamstring stretch. If you can't reach the ankle, try the calf, the back of the knee, or the upper quadriceps—whatever you can comfortably reach. In addition to stretching the

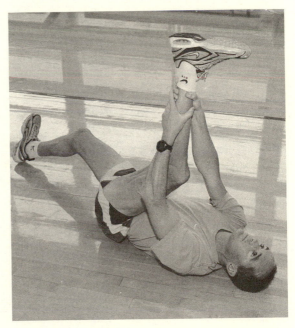

Buttocks stretch number three.

buttocks, this will also stretch part of the upper hamstring. Repeat the entire sequence, of course, with the other leg. It's OK to bend the knee, as in the photo below opposite. Repeat the entire sequence, of course, with the other leg.

> **There's no need to hold a stretch for more than a few seconds, and there's virtually no benefit from repeating the same stretch more than once.**

Upper-Body Stretches

You're not likely to get a running injury by failing to stretch out the upper body, but as long as you're in a stretching mood, why not take a few more seconds to complete the job? Here's a three-stretch drill that will limber up your arms and shoulders in about a minute. If you sometimes put in intense sessions on a computer, this drill may do you even more good during office breaks than for running warm-ups.

Begin by clasping your hands behind your back. Keeping your arms straight at the elbows, extend them backward, feeling the stretch mostly in the front of your shoulders.

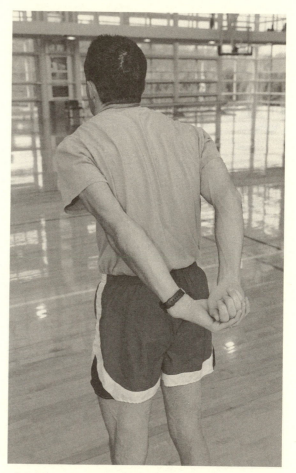

Shoulder stretch number one.

Shoulder stretch number two.

For the second stretch, unclasp your hands and wrap one arm—in this example, the right arm—around the front of your body, under your chin to reach over the top of the other shoulder as though you were trying to scratch

STRETCHING DOS AND DON'TS

1. *Do* make stretching a regular part of your fitness routine.

2. *Do* stretch at least as many times a week as you run.

3. *Don't* overcommit. A five-minute routine that actually fits your workout schedule is better than a grandiose plan that never happens.

4. *Do* stretch until you feel a pleasant pull to the muscle.

5. *Don't* do bouncing stretches or stretch to the point of pain.

6. *Do* include gentle stretching as part of an injury-rehabilitation program (see chapter 9 on aches and pains), but be very careful not to aggravate the injury by overstretching the injured tissues.

7. *Don't* do the traditional hamstring stretch unless you're a serious competitor and have received individual expert advice.

a hard-to-reach itch. Park the hand flat on your shoulder blade, or as close to that as you can comfortably reach. The right elbow should now be sticking out in front of your chin. Place your left hand on the back of the right elbow or on the lower part of the upper arm, and gently pull as though attempting to wrap the right arm tighter around your body.

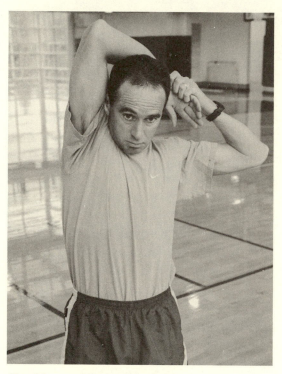

The third stretch begins by reaching the right arm over the top of your head, more or less getting your hand within scratching distance of your left shoulder. Grasp your right wrist with your free hand and rock your head, neck, and torso to the left to stretch your side and a new group of shoulder muscles. Switch arms and repeat all three stretches.

Congratulations, you're finished.

Shoulder stretch number three.

WEIGHT TRAINING AND
CROSS-TRAINING

B Y THE TIME YOU'VE built up to three 20-minute runs a week, you should consider adding weight training to your running program. Not only will as little as 30 minutes of weight training a week help tone your entire body, but it will add strength to your legs, which in turn will help you run faster and more comfortably.

Running coaches once believed that all that you needed to do to strengthen your body for running was to run. But it's been shown that runners who lift weights are stronger and better runners—as well as in better overall condition—than those who don't. This is because weight lifting allows you to isolate specific muscles and stress them heavily in brief but intense workouts.

More importantly, weight lifting can be used to strengthen muscles like the abdominals and shoulders that don't get much exercise during running but that help maintain proper running posture. Keeping these muscles strong will help prevent backaches, stiff necks, and tired shoulders. Weight lifting can also reduce your susceptibility to injury and can even cure specific injuries, such as shin splints or runner's knee, which are often associated with specific muscle weaknesses.

Chapter 9 discusses how weight lifting can be focused on these and other specific injuries. Here we address weight *training*, which involves a regular weekly program designed more for prevention and overall health than for the elimination of specific problems.

Bodybuilding isn't the goal. Although you'll add some muscle mass, you won't turn into a Schwarzenegger clone on the limited program outlined below. As a runner, in fact, excessive bulking up is counterproductive because you then would have to carry all that muscle around with you on each workout.

The effect of weight lifting comes from the combination of the amount of weight you lift and the number of times (*repetitions* or *reps* in the jargon of the weight room) that you lift it. Each group of reps, with an intervening rest break, is called a *set*. There's nothing magic about the order in which you do the exercises or the precise amount of time you take to recover between sets. You do, however, need at least a 60-second rest break between sets, and you will probably feel you're getting a better workout if you let no more than five minutes elapse between sets. But you don't have to stand around doing nothing during the recovery intervals; you'll generally have plenty of energy to move directly from one muscle group to another. For exercises that work one leg at a time, you may find that you can rattle off two or three sets in fairly rapid-fire succession simply by alternating legs.

HEAVY BREATHING

Holding your breath—the beginning weight lifter's natural tendency—causes a buildup in pressure in the chest as the rib cage is squeezed by your exertions. This can cut off blood flow to the heart—an obviously bad idea. With the light weights you'll be using, this is a low risk, but it's still good to practice safe lifting methods: exhale as you lift; inhale when lowering the weight back to rest.

It's also a good idea to warm up on a treadmill, exercise bike, or by vigorous walking before lifting. With the relatively light weights I recommend, muscle pulls are rare, but why chance it?

Power lifters puff and strain to heave close to the maximum possible weight skyward with each repetition. They'll rarely accomplish more than five of these lifts per set. Your purposes are better served by doing more reps with smaller weights. Choose the weights so you can do 12 to 15 reps per set. This will result in a lot less grunting and a lot less of the muscular protests that power lifters call "a good burn." Don't worry about feeling like a wimp, lifting your light weights in a gym populated by power lifters. They'll know, watching your longer series of reps, that you're seeking different goals.

Old-school weightlifting wisdom recommends doing three sets each time you work out, with three workouts a week for each muscle group. But you can do less and still get most of the benefit. In fact, three times a week is slightly too often; the best research indicates that you'll get better results if you work each set of muscles every third day. And unless you're trying to rehabilitate an injury or are following a doctor-prescribed recovery from surgery, working out twice a week should be adequate.

> **Weight lifting can reduce your susceptibility to injury and can even cure specific injuries, such as shin splints or runner's knee.**

Nor do you need to do the traditional three sets. Studies have shown that you get at least 90 percent of the benefit from doing only two. Dropping to one set, however, probably reduces the benefit by nearly half.

Power lifters raise and lower each weight slowly, concentrating on the muscle as they flex it, and then gradually release it. You can do this if you want, but it's not mandatory for your purposes. Just don't pump the weights so quickly that you risk pulling a muscle. And make sure you work the muscle on both parts of the cycle, lifting and lowering. With the light weights you should be using, each set of 15 will take about 25 to 30 seconds. You might get slightly more benefit if you slow the rhythm down a bit, but unless you're a seriously competitive runner, the extra time probably isn't worth it.

When beginning, make sure to err on the light side when choosing what weights to lift. It's amazingly easy to work yourself so hard in a few minutes that you have a memorable set of sore muscles for days afterward. You'll be a lot happier if you're conservative, adding a little more weight with each workout until you've learned what you can comfortably lift. As with running, your progress won't be seen overnight, but within a month you should be noticing that you're more comfortable with heavier weights than you were at the beginning. If you want, you can keep a log of the weights lifted and the numbers of reps and sets, but all you really need to keep track of are the dates on which you've worked out and whether those workouts affected the upper body, the lower body, or both.

As with other types of training, weight training strengthens muscles by tearing them down slightly so that the body rebuilds them stronger than before. Because it's more intense than running, however, you need a longer recovery period, which is why you shouldn't lift more often than every third day. If you want to visit the gym more frequently, try alternating between upper- and lower-body workouts. Most beginners, however, will probably find it more efficient to work out less frequently and do everything all at once. You can run and lift on the same day, but you will probably be more comfortable if you run first.

There are two basic types of weights: free weights (barbells and dumbbells) and machines. Athletes in sports like basketball, football, and baseball prefer free weights because they force you to develop greater balance. They also build strength connections among related muscle groups. But these connections are needed only in sports that draw on explosive bursts of co-ordinated power. You can get your job done with either type of weights, but working solely with free weights takes a good deal longer. The program presented in this chapter therefore works mostly with machines.

Strength training is easiest if you have access to a well-equipped health club or gym. On your own, you might be able to do a partial workout via calisthenics such as push-ups, pull-ups, lunges, squats, and abdominal curls, but it's difficult to find calisthenic-style exercises that isolate important muscles in the legs, such as the hamstrings. You may, however, be able to get a pretty good workout from an all-in-one machine. I've never tried one, but as long as they're well constructed and exercise the right muscles, there's no reason they shouldn't work.

Another alternative is to do some of your leg excersises with ankle weights. These are definitely useful for rehabilitating an injury, but for regular hamstring or quadriceps workouts, the amount of weight needed could easily become impractical. Even if you can find heavy enough weights, ankle weights won't do as good a job as weight-room machines do of helping you isolate the muscles you're trying to exercise.

Rubber tubing may provide a better solution for those without access to a weight room, but rubber-tubing exercises are beyond the scope of this book. In setting up a home tubing workout station, make sure the tube ends are fastened securely enough so they don't come loose and give you a memorable slap.

BASIC LOWER-BODY EXERCISES

At a minimum, there are three weightlifting exercises you need to do for your lower body. These are designed to exercise the quadriceps, the hamstrings, and the calves.

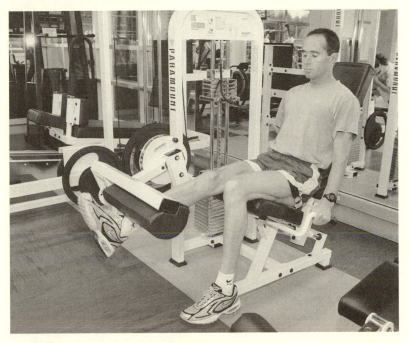

Quadriceps extension.

Quadriceps Extension. The quads are the big muscles on the fronts of your thighs. The best way to strengthen them is on specially designed machines, where you sit with a padded bar across the top of your feet. Using one leg, raise the bar until your leg is nearly straight, but don't lock the knee. Locking the knee puts heavy stress on the tendons around the kneecap, risking injury. Although it doubles the amount of time you spend on the machine, the only way (on most machines) to be sure you're exercising both legs equally is to work them in separate sets. At the bottom of the cycle, however, your quads are in their weakest position, and you may need an assist from the resting leg. Do so to first lift the weight off its blocks, then avoid the need in subsequent reps by not lowering the weight all the way back down until you've finished the set. In fact, try to bend your knee no more than 45 degrees between lifts; repeatedly lifting from a lower position can be hard on your knees.

Hamstring curl.

Hamstring curl. The machine for hamstring curls has you lie on your stomach, with a padded bar behind your ankles. Again, you may need to use both legs to raise the bar for the first few inches without overstraining, but after that you should exercise each hamstring separately, lowering the bar no farther than you can easily raise it back up with one leg.

Calf raise. Calf raises can be done at a health club, on a sidewalk curb, or at home. All you need is a step, with something nearby to hold onto for balance. Stand with your heels hanging out over empty air; then alternately drop your heels as far as they will comfortably go and rise up

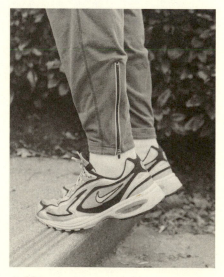
Calf raise.

on your toes to the top of your comfortable range of motion. Because you're lifting only your own body weight, this exercise will be relatively easy. Compensate by building up to sets of 30, doing 10 reps with your toes pointed straight ahead, 10 with toes outward, and 10 with toes angled inward. That sounds like a lot of reps, but each takes only a second or two.

Optional Lower-Body Exercises

There are lots of other lower-body exercises, but four of the best are lunges, squats, dead lifts, and leg raises.

Lunge.

Lunge. Start from a standing position, with your feet about shoulder-width apart. From this position, step forward, dipping your front knee toward the floor like a fencer on the attack, keeping your torso straight. If the phrase that runs through your mind is *en garde*, you're probably making the right motion. Unlike the fencer, however, do this with your arms immobile, hands on hips. There's some exercise from the forward lunge, but most of the work comes from standing back up from this bent-knee position. The amount depends on the combination of how far you step forward and how deeply you bend your knee. Start easy, and never bend the knee more than 90 degrees. As you progress, you can increase the exercise by stepping farther forward, dipping the knee more deeply, and (eventually) carrying dumbbells in your hands or a weight bar across your shoulders.

Squat. These can be done standing while holding dumbbells. But you've got more control on a leg press machine that has you lie on your back, with your feet pressed against an elevated plate. Straightening your legs shoves the plate forward (or your body backward), lifting an attached stack of weights. To avoid knee

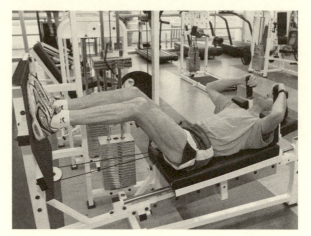

Leg press.

strain, position your torso so your knees are never bent more than 90 degrees; some experts advise against bending your knees more than 45 degrees.

Dead lift. The dead lift is a classic lift, but it shouldn't be attempted by people with back problems. Nor is it an exercise for macho endeavors to determine the maximum amount you can lift. The lift itself is simple. Set the weight bar down on the floor; then bend over to grasp it, making sure your knees are bent enough that your torso never has to lean forward more than 45 degrees. Lift the bar by standing back upright, raising the weight with your legs more than with your back, as when picking up any heavy object. The primary purpose of this exercise isn't to strengthen your back muscles; it's to work the top part of your hamstrings. Even so, if you have a history of back problems, you shouldn't attempt this lift without first talking to a doctor, trainer, or physical therapist. After each repetition, lower the weight back to (or near) the floor with the same bent-legged posture you used to lift it.

Dead lift.

Leg raise.

Leg raise. This is another classic exercise that you probably did in grade school. It's for the lower abdominal muscles, not the legs, but since it's the legs that move, I've grouped it with lower-body exercises. Lying on your back, lift your straight legs so the heels are a few inches off the floor. To reduce strain on your back, tighten your stomach muscles before you begin, flattening your spine against the floor. But if you have a bad back, consult with a physical therapist or professional trainer before attempting this exercise.

SAFETY TIPS

If in doubt about how to do any of these exercises, ask for a demonstration from a trainer at your gym or health club; the best way to learn is by watching someone else. Also, health clubs typically post detailed instructions near each machine.

Never lift weights without warming up for a few minutes, perhaps by walking briskly on a treadmill or spinning gently on an exercise bicycle. I've never pulled a muscle in a weight room, but it's possible with cold muscles, and it's a really silly way to temporarily disable yourself. Five minutes of warm-up should be sufficient—just enough that you begin to sweat a bit.

If an exercise causes any pain other than the normal "burn" of a well-worked muscle, stop immediately and consult an expert. You may be doing something wrong, or you may have a physical condition that makes it unwise to do that particular exercise. For the same reasons, start any new exercise at a weight that feels relatively easy, until you're sure your body can handle it.

UPPER-BODY EXERCISES

For runners, exercising the upper body is mostly a matter of working the major muscle groups enough to give you good overall muscle tone. If you're also a bicyclist or a cross-country skier, or if you are planning to lug big backpacks around the wilderness, you may also want to beef up your upper-body training to focus on each of these activities, particularly at the start of

Crunches.

each season. Most of the exercises described below are traditional and will serve multiple purposes.

There are only two upper-body exercises that should be considered mandatory for runners: crunches and back raises. **Crunches** are the successor to the sit-ups you probably learned in grade school. The difference is that you focus the exercise more strongly on your abdominal muscles by not actually sitting all the way up. Lie on your back, knees bent, feet on the floor. Initially, the exercise is almost static, as you tighten your abdominal muscles and flatten your spine against the floor. As you gain strength, curl your head and shoulders upward to increase the resistance. You can do crunches in sets of 15, just like any other weightlifting exercise, or you can simply build up to a single large set of perhaps 50.

Back raise.

Back raises can be done on special machines or by simply lying on a padded mat. As with dead lifts, if you're prone to back problems, don't do back raises without first consulting a back specialist. This exercise is like a reverse crunch. Lie on your stomach, with your hands clasped behind the small of your back. Using the back muscles, curl your head and shoulders an inch or two above the mat, being careful to avoid overstraining. As you gain strength, you can increase resistance noticeably by clasping your hands behind your neck rather than behind your back.

The rest of your upper-body workout can involve any combination of lat pulls, biceps curls, push-ups, or triceps extensions. As a runner, you need not be as worried about minor upper-body imbalances as you should be about exercising your legs equally, so there's no reason to devote separate sets to

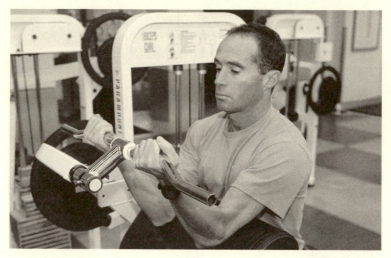

Biceps curl.

each arm. Nevertheless, you should do your best to exercise them equally. Following are a few suggested exercises.

Biceps curl. Running doesn't make much use of the biceps, so if your goal is overall muscle tone, this is one of your more important supplemental exercises. It can be done on a specialty machine or with free weights. Either way, you simply lift the desired weight by flexing your biceps.

Triceps extension. The triceps is the muscle on the side of the upper arm opposite the biceps. The biceps flexes the

This triceps machine has a weighted bar that arcs from behind my head to this elevated position.

arm; the triceps straightens it. In running, your arm swing makes more use of the triceps than the biceps. The easiest way to isolate the triceps for weight lifting is with a triceps extension machine. But you can also do it with free weights by putting the weight bar behind your neck, with your elbows pointing out in front of you. Without moving the elbows, swing the bar upward until your arms are straight, raised above your head.

Lat pull-down.

Lat pull-down. These are best done with a machine that uses a chain or a strap to suspend a bar over your head. Grasping the bar by its handgrips, pull it downward until it reaches the bottom of your neck. To exercise slightly different groups of shoulder muscles, do sets in pairs, pulling the bar down behind your head for one and in front of your head for the other.

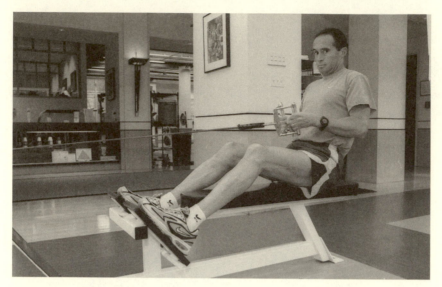

Lat rowing pull. Sit up straight, and work your arms and shoulders, not your back.

Lat rowing pull. Another pulling exercise, this one is done horizontally rather than vertically. The simplest machines are similar to the pull-down machines, with a bar you pull toward your chest while sitting on a bench. Make sure you pull with your arms and shoulders, not your back. More complex machines seat you in a chair that braces your torso to isolate the proper shoulder muscles. Health-club staff can show you how to use these machines. Doing lat rowing pulls isn't the same thing as working out on a rowing machine; those machines use both the arms and legs at a much lower level of intensity. Rowing machines should be considered part of cross-training (see pages 124–25), not weight lifting.

Butterfly curl. Aptly named, these exercises strengthen the pectorals. Sitting in a comfortable, supportive chair, you reach to the sides to place your elbows behind a metal bar, which has an extension that you also grasp with your hands. At this point, there's only one way to move, which is to use your chest muscles to swing your arms toward each other in front of you—like an enormous butterfly flapping its wings. A foot pedal helps you get started from the initial wings-open position, where your pecs are too weak to lift much weight.

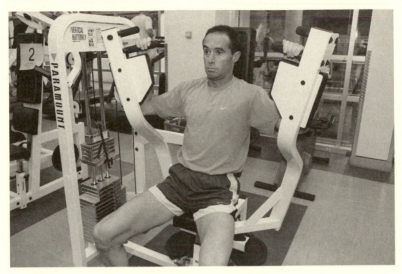

Butterfly curl.

EFFICIENT LIFTING

Weight lifting for fitness runners is designed to supplement your running program, not as a major task in and of itself. Basically, you just want to reach the point where you're feeling a good workout. It isn't rocket science. Although 15 repetitions per set is the usual target, there's not much difference between that and doing 12 reps at slightly higher weights.

WEIGHT ROOM ETIQUETTE

Weight rooms can be intimidating to beginners. A few simple rules, however, will ensure that you're welcome.

1. Don't bang down the weights. That damages equipment, eventually breaking it.
2. Don't hog the machines. Rather than sitting on one machine, waiting to recover enough to do your next set, move to a different exercise, freeing the first machine for the next user.
3. Wipe down the equipment after you use it as a courtesy to the next user.

With practice, you can become efficient at whipping through your routine, moving from station to station with little wasted time. If one machine is in use, alter the order, rather than wasting time waiting. I have my own gym equipment, so crowding is never a problem, but without feeling hurried I can get through the recommended lower-body workout—including the optional exercises—in about 5 minutes a set. That's 10 minutes for the full workout if you're doing two sets; 15 minutes if you choose to do three. The full upper-body workout takes longer if you do all seven exercises, but if you pick only a few and limit yourself to two sets, you can do it in about 7 or 8 minutes. That's a small price to pay twice a week for substantial benefits both to running and to overall fitness.

Now that I'm no longer running competitively, I make sure I give my lower body two complete rest days a week. Those days off substantially reduce the risk of injury and give me more pep when I return to running.

CROSS-TRAINING

The term *cross-training* is coaching jargon for investing part of your training in a sport other than your principal one. Reasons to cross-train vary. Some people want to exercise a different set of muscles; others seek activities that closely mimic their main sports for occasions when their first love is impossible. Cross-country skiers, for example, need cross-training to keep in shape during the snow-free months.

Elite runners don't do much cross-training, unless you broaden the definition to include weight lifting and stretching—which are better viewed as parts of your core training. If your goal is to become the best possible runner, the most efficient way to train is by running as much as your body will tolerate.

As a fitness runner, however, your objective is different, and you can get the same cardiovascular benefits from any activity that gives you the desired 20- to 30-minute increase in heart rate. Such workouts give you a way to vary your routine or increase your exercise level without increased pounding. They may also be fun, and the cardiovascular fitness you've obtained from running will carry over to them, making them easier than would otherwise be the case.

Bicycling is probably the most popular form of cross-training, partly because, like running, it can be done conveniently from your doorstep. Other options include the following:

- swimming
- stair climbing
- stationary cycling
- using a rowing machine
- hiking
- cross-country skiing
- vigorous yard work

Just remember that none of these sports uses exactly the same set of muscles as running, which means you need to be careful not to hurt yourself by taking them up too quickly. For the same reason, if you want cross-training workouts to be comfortable, they need to be done fairly regularly, or you'll never adapt. You can get a spectacular workout splitting firewood or shoveling snow, for example, but if you only do so a few times a year, you can also get some impressively sore muscles.

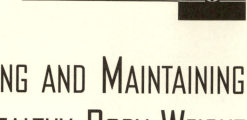

ACHIEVING AND MAINTAINING
HEALTHY BODY WEIGHT

ONE OF THE MOST popular reasons for taking up running—or any other form of exercise—is to shed a few pounds of accumulated weight. And it's no surprise: running can burn anywhere from 500 to 1,000 calories an hour, depending on how big you are and how fast you run. Brisk walking, by way of contrast, burns about 300 to 400 calories an hour.

But you need to be realistic. Running by itself won't melt off 50 excess pounds overnight. Fat has about 3,500 calories per pound, so to burn off 10 pounds by running, you would have to run 35 to 70 hours.

Before you let that statistic depress you too much, however, consider the following factors.

1. The American Heart Association and other cardiovascular health experts have learned that shedding as few as 5 to 10 pounds can measurably reduce your risk of heart disease. And these studies focus only on the benefit of weight loss; trimming down by running improves cardiovascular fitness in ways that are even more important. Running an hour a week, you can achieve this initial 5- to 10-pound target in 6 to 12 months, without changing your diet. Running for 30 minutes a day five days a week will cut weight more than twice as quickly.

2. With time, these 5- and 10-pound increments begin to add up. Running 20 minutes a day three days a week translates to running off nearly a pound every month for the indefinite future.

3. You may be able to lose weight faster by crash diets than by exercise, but that's because those diets tend to burn muscle rather than fat. Since muscle has only 1,600 calories per pound, muscle atrophy cuts weight twice as quickly as fat burning—deluding you into thinking you're making rapid progress. Actually, you're just wasting away your strength. Exercising while losing weight will help you lose more fat and less muscle, as long as you obey the rules of proper nutrition shown on pages 136–37.

4. Exercise is a good way to maintain a weight loss that you've achieved by other means, such as dieting. You don't need to have much experience at dieting to know that it's relatively easy to lose weight: it's keeping it off that's the challenge. In 1992, the U.S. National Institutes of Health (NIH) estimated that the average person who loses weight solely by dieting regains perhaps two-thirds of it within the first year—and virtually all of it in five years. And we've all known people who've spent months slimming down, only to rebound afterward to wind up even heavier than when they started. Even liposuction patients, who've invested thousands of dollars and the pain of surgery in their initial losses, often rebound.

   Exercise, however, can alter these outcomes—enough so that the NIH calls exercise "essential" both to better overall health and to long-term weight-loss maintenance. Simply stated, running can play a major role in keeping you from regaining all the lost weight—or possibly more—after dieting.

EXERCISING AND DIETING

Regular exercise, especially running, is crucial for maintaining permanent weight loss. Rick is a good case in point.

"By dieting, I shed 55 pounds the year before I met Alberto, then got back into running after years away from it. A year after I started running, I weighed precisely what I did when I ended the diet—and I credit exercise with my success."

WEIGHT THEORY

Contrary to popular impression, the weight creep that afflicts so many Americans isn't caused by periodic dinnertime pig-outs. Nor is it caused by persistent gluttony. Weight-loss researchers have noted that the steady, pound-or-two-per-year gain that afflicts so many people translates to only 10 to 20 calories a day. That's about the number of calories in one carrot (or one tortilla chip) a day, an imbalance that's impossible to spot in the overall diet. Yet it can add up to 30 to 60 pounds of flab over the course of three decades.

> **In my racing days, when I was training 15 to 17 miles a day, I was probably eating close to 4,000 to 5,000 calories a day.**

An apple-a-day imbalance—still too small to be spotted by anyone but a nutrition researcher—will add up to nearly a pound a month. Yes, some people are bingers or depression eaters who down a gallon of ice cream at a sitting, but most overweight people have had the weight come on so slowly that their average diets don't look perceptibly different from anyone else's.

So if overindulgence isn't the problem, what really is going on? Increasingly, nutrition researchers are coming to believe that the body employs a complex feedback mechanism to set its target weight. If it thinks it's starving, it reduces its metabolic rate and initiates food cravings that make it harder to resist your favorite high-calorie temptations, whether they be chips, candy bars, or fast-food hamburgers. If the body feels oversatiated, it shuts off these cravings and turns up the metabolic rate a bit to burn off some unwanted fat. It's clearly a survival pattern left over from our remote ancestors' feast-or-famine lifestyles as hunter-gatherers.

Scientists at Oregon Health Science University in Portland recently announced that they had found the part of the brain that controls this feedback mechanism in mice, dubbing it the *adipostat*—a combination of the terms *adipose* ("fat") and *thermostat* (*Neuron*, Sept. 1999). Finding and understanding the equivalent structure in humans, they hope, will someday go a long way toward unraveling the mysteries of weight creep.

But the basic problem is that the body doesn't necessarily set a healthy target weight, and that the target weight it does set has a tendency to creep upward with age. This is why crash diets rarely produce long-term success. By sudden clampdowns of the will, they can indeed cut weight, but they do nothing to alter the adipostat. After the diet's over, your body thinks it's starving and it tries every way it can to regain its lost reserves. Each time you get distracted, it snags a few extra calories. Your weight ratchets up a notch, until pretty soon you're back where you started—or higher. It's not a character flaw: it's biochemical treason.

Obviously, the goal is to reset the adipostat to a lower target weight. And until someone understands the adipostat well enough to invent a safe dial-a-weight pill, high-intensity exercise may be the best way to do that.

You can't safely start up a running program at an intense enough level to feel the overnight effects on appetite. But even a modest amount of running appears to reset the adipostat in ways that make weight, once lost, less likely to return. And running is something that most people can build into their normal work schedules.

In my racing days, when I was training 15 to 17 miles a day, I was probably going through close to 4,000 to 5,000 calories a day—about double the normal person's diet. At that level of intake, it's theoretically possible to gain weight, but most elite runners find that they're eating all day long just trying to keep up. I used to wake up hungry at 2 A.M., needing a couple of bowls of cereal as a snack—and that was after a large dinner.

Today, running about 30 miles a week and doing some cycling, I have to be more careful. But I'm still burning off about 500 calories a day more than I would if I were sedentary. That means I can still have a scoop of ice cream or some other treat that I'd otherwise have to pass up.

BODY MASS INDEX: THE NEW HEIGHT-WEIGHT MEASURE

To determine your ideal weight, start by using your height and weight to calculate your *body mass index* (BMI). It's easy to do if you work in metric units, or you can work in pounds and inches and remember an odd conversion factor.

Your BMI is simply your weight in kilograms divided by the square of your height in meters. As a mathematical formula, that would be stated as

$$BMI = \frac{\text{weight in kilograms}}{(\text{height in meters})^2}$$

I'm 1.88 meters tall and weighed 65 kilograms during my racing days. That gave me a BMI of 18.4—far on the lean side. Today, at 73 kilograms, my BMI is 20.6, still near the bottom of the "normal" range (see below). To convert from English units, divide your weight in pounds by 2.2 and divide your height in inches by 39.4. Or, you can do the whole thing in English units (pounds and inches) and multiply by 691 to make the unit changes automatically.

$$BMI = \frac{(\text{weight in pounds}) \times 691}{(\text{height in inches})^2}$$

A "normal" BMI is about 20 to 25, which is a fairly broad range. If you're fine boned, you'll probably look and feel best at the lower end of the range; if you're large boned, you'll want to be at the upper end. Average-boned people will be closer to the middle. Find out which category you fit by encircling one wrist with the other hand. If your thumb and longest finger overlap, you're fine boned. If they barely touch, you're average, and if there's a gap between them, you're large-boned. Even if you're currently overweight, this test should still work because most people don't put on weight in their wrists.

These target weight ranges vary somewhat, regardless of your bone structure. A fine-boned bodybuilder is going to be heavier than a heavy-boned person who has never wanted to bulk up. If your BMI is in the 20 to 25 range, you're considered normal, regardless of bone structure. A BMI below 18 is definitely considered "underweight."

A BMI of 25 or above, however, is the medical definition of being overweight. And a BMI of 30 or above is the clinical definition of obesity. A few muscle-bound hulks may have BMIs over 25 without carrying significant excess fat, but most people will definitely feel better and be healthier by cutting back. The chart at right shows normal, overweight, and clinically obese weight levels for a wide range of heights.

BMI-BASED WEIGHTS BY HEIGHT

BMI HEIGHT[1]	20 BMI[2]	25 BMI[3]	30 BMI[4]
4'11"	101 lb.	126 lb.	151 lb.
5'0"	104	130	156
5'1"	108	135	162
5'2"	111	139	167
5'3"	115	144	172
5'4"	119	148	178
5'5"	122	153	183
5'6"	126	158	189
5'7"	130	162	195
5'8"	134	167	201
5'9"	138	172	207
5'10"	142	177	213
5'11"	146	182	219
6'0"	150	188	225
6'1"	154	193	231
6'2"	158	198	238
6'3"	163	204	244
6'4"	167	209	251
6'5"	172	215	257
6'6"	176	220	264

[1] People outside this height range can use the formula on page 130.

[2] Low end of "normal" range.

[3] High end of "normal" range; higher weights are classified as "overweight."

[4] Clinical definition of obesity.

A SIMPLE FORMULA FOR SHEDDING POUNDS

Healthy weight loss is based on a simple formula.

$$\text{pounds of fat lost} = \frac{(\text{calories expended}) - (\text{calories eaten})}{3,500}$$

Yes, you can lose weight more quickly than 3,500 calories per pound by "sweating it off" or burning muscle, but both of these methods are counterproductive. Your body needs to be fully hydrated to function properly; if you keep your weight down by being perpetually dehydrated, you're just trying to fool the scales, creating one problem (dehydration) to mask another (your true weight). You're better off to stay hydrated and face the weight problem directly. Losing muscle is also to be avoided if possible. Realistically, it's almost impossible to lose a significant amount of weight without losing some muscle mass, but it's best to think entirely in terms of fat and resign yourself to that 3,500 calorie-per-pound figure.

Don't try to lose more than 2 pounds per week. If you do, you'll almost certainly shed most of it in unhealthy manners. Diets that promise magic ways of losing 30 pounds in 30 days, for example, are either dehydrating you or losing all of the weight in muscle—or both. Steer clear of these diets.

> **Diets promising magic ways of losing 30 pounds in 30 days are either dehydrating you or losing all of the weight in muscle—or both.**

The fat-burning equation gives you control of three factors, two of which are influenced by exercise. The factor not related to exercise is your calorie intake. Unfortunately, most people do not count calories correctly. Nutrition researchers regularly observe that people claim to be eating about two-thirds as many calories as they actually are, either because they fail to remember everything they eat or because they just don't realize how calorie-dense some foods actually are. Although some people are indeed metabolic oddities who eat like birds and gain weight, most of those who say, for example, "I gain weight anytime I eat more than 1,300 calories a day," actually are eating about 2,000 calories—which is what the average, inactive person really does need for weight maintenance.

Some diet programs, such as Weight Watchers, finesse their participants' calorie-counting difficulties by having them count servings of such foods as breads, fruits, meats, and vegetables. But for long-term weight maintenance, it helps to be able to count calories—and to train yourself to add up what you've eaten midway through the day. Read nutrition labels, invest in a book of calorie tables, and weigh suspect portions whenever possible on diet scales. After a while, you'll be able to eyeball a cookie or muffin and say, "Egads, that thing's got at least 600 calories!"—a realization that is often instrumental to leaving it for someone else.

Detailed calorie counting is beyond the scope of this book, but it pays to recognize the following.

- Carbohydrates and protein have about 100 calories per dry ounce (about 4 calories per gram). Water, of course, has none.
- Fat has about 250 calories per ounce (9 calories per gram).
- "Percent fat-free" labeling is misleading. Whole milk is 96-percent fat free, but it's almost 50-percent fat (most of the rest is water). The same goes for lots of other foods with high water contents. Read the nutrition labels to avoid being fooled.
- Nonfat foods still have calories. They're great as substitutes for higher-fat foods, but you can't eat endless quantities of them.
- A trend toward large-size packaging has led to candy bars and luncheon bags of chips containing 400 to 500 calories—20 to 25 percent of an entire day's caloric needs for the average person. They're often labeled as two or three servings, but how often do you eat only half of a candy bar? Calculate the calories in the entire package before you buy, and presume you'll eat the whole thing unless you're sure you'll be sharing it.
- Remember that there's no such thing as a "bad food." Dietary imbalance and weight gain come from having too much of otherwise acceptable foods. If you have a sweet tooth, you may be able to satisfy it nearly as well with an after-dinner mint as with a candy bar, with a huge difference in the number of calories.
- If you're not losing weight as quickly as expected, search your diet for hidden calories, particularly fat, which can skulk in unexpected places, particularly in packaged food or restaurant cooking.

The exercise-dependent variables in the fat-burning equation are exercise itself and your daily maintenance calories, sometimes called your *base metabolic rate*. Combined, they determine your total calorie expenditure. ___ will burn about 100 calories a mile for the average runner, male ___ t doesn't matter how fast you run: the difference in calorie ex-___ etween running at a world-class pace and a slow jog—or even a brisk walk—is mostly related to *the number of miles you can cover in 20 or 30 minutes—not the speed at which they're run* (in other words, the racer and the jogger burn off different numbers of calories per hour, but nearly the same amount per mile). Nor does it matter much whether you're unusually large or small; per-mile calorie expenditures tend to fall between 95 and 125 calories per mile, regardless of body type.

DRAMATIC RESULTS

The results of increased exercise can, in fact, be dramatic. Rick notes that when he was overweight, his appetite immediately reduced when he was on a long backpacking trip. It was as though his body would say, "Hey, dummy, you weigh too much to be doing all this work!" and then would set about cutting weight as fast as it could. Backpacking 10 miles a day, Rick would want no more food than he did in daily life back home. Now that he's lost weight, however, he finds that active vacations *increase* his appetite, as his body seeks to avoid becoming too thin.

If you're counting calories, you need to have a rough estimate of the distance you're running. Visit a high school track, and run a mile at your normal jogging pace. Or, measure one of your usual running courses with a car or bicycle odometer and figure out your average pace. Then use that pace to estimate how much distance you cover per workout (see page 173–74). Precision isn't necessary.

When you're starting your running program, these calorie-expenditure numbers may seem depressingly small: six minutes of running/walking is unlikely to cover even half a mile. But remember, as we discussed in chapter 2, that your goals are long-term: if you build all the way up to 30 minutes five times a week, you may well be running 15 miles or more a week. That's enough mileage to make a noticeable impact on your waistline.

Exercise gives a second dividend by increasing your base metabolic rate for a few hours afterward. This base metabolic rate, in fact, is what many of the potions, herbs, and popular "fat melting" diet regimens claim to adjust. Some may even work, but the impacts are probably not as large as the hype suggests. Researchers in Switzerland, for example, recently asked volunteer subjects to spend time in airtight hotel rooms, where the study team could determine precisely how much oxygen they consumed—a direct measure of their metabolic rates. These researchers were interested in the impact of green tea, which many see as a promising metabolic booster. They found that on the days when the volunteers consumed tea their metabolisms ran about 100 calories higher than on days when they didn't.

It's my guess that many other metabolism-influencing factors, including exercise, are similar: they boost your metabolism, but probably by no more than about 100 calories a day. If so, their short-term "fat-melting" benefits are largely oversold. But remember how a 10- to 20-calorie-a-day imbalance can create a 60-pound weight creep over the course of decades? If exercise increases your base metabolism by as little as 50 to 100 calories a day—*and you don't compensate by increasing your eating*—you'll creep back downward by a pound every one or two months, a very nice bonus indeed.

High-Protein Diets

Popular diets come and go, but one that has persisted for several years is the high-protein, low-carbohydrate diet, popularized in slightly different forms by Robert C. Atkins and Barry Sears.

These diets are based on the theory that calories per se aren't your enemy; that role is reserved for carbohydrates. The reasoning and specific dietary advice differ, but such diets encourage you to eat high-fat, high-protein meals and to avoid breads, pasta, fruits, and starchy vegetables, except perhaps for one meal a day.

In the short run, these diets clearly work: people do indeed use them to lose significant quantities of weight. But they fly in the face of traditional athletic diets, which view carbohydrates as your primary fuel (see page 138). And they make nutritionists nervous because they're imbalanced. Grains carry important vitamins, and fruits are good for fighting everything from constipation to cancer.

Nutritionists aren't the only ones who are concerned about these diets; cardiologists note that they abound in fat and cholesterol. The bottom line: they may work in the short run, but they're not a great long-term lifestyle.

Successful Losers: 3,000 People Can't Be Wrong

Since 1993, researchers in Denver and Pittsburgh have been compiling a database of more than 3,000 successful weight losers, tracking their progress annually. The purpose of the database, called the National Weight Control

Registry, is to determine the keys to these people's success. Study participants must have lost at least 30 pounds and have kept it off for at least a year.

The people in the study initially lost weight by a variety of means, but there is remarkable homogeneity in the way they've maintained their losses. Most, for example, are following low-fat diets—and virtually none are now on the high-fat, high-protein Atkins or Sears diets. But at the same time, these successful losers haven't bought into the popular belief that just because a food is low in fat, they can eat unlimited quantities of it.

Most importantly, members of the database are remarkably dedicated exercisers, reporting that they work out not just the 30 minutes a day recommended by most health experts, but as much as one or two hours a day, despite conventionally busy schedules.

So if you've lost weight and are trying to hold it off with exercise, take heart: there are thousands of people out there just like you who've beaten the odds. Most of the exercisers in the database are walkers. As a runner, you've got an advantage: you can pack as much exercise into 30 minutes as most walkers do into an hour—making it correspondingly easier to find time.

FOOD OR FUEL: NUTRITION BASICS

Few topics are more emotionally laden than food is. Headlines rage about genetically modified food crops, pesticide residues, and the benefits or lack thereof of the latest nutritional supplements. Vegetarians and carnivores square off over the dinner table, and health advocates alternately sway huge followings or are denigrated as "nutrition police." French gastronomist Anthelme Brillat-Savarin had it right a long time ago with the now-famous pronouncement: "Tell me what you eat and I will tell you who you are." The only thing missed by that proverb (usually condensed to "You are what you eat") is the degree to which people divide into warring dietary camps.

Nutrition for fitness runners isn't a great deal different from nutrition for anyone else. You need a balanced diet, with lots of fruits and vegetables, and low-fat meats—pretty much the same things that everyone recommends for health. Fiber is also good: most Americans eat only half the fiber that nutritionists recommend. When possible, eat whole-grain breads rather than highly refined grains, and drink water or fruit juice rather than soda pop. A balanced diet may not help you run better, but study after study has shown that low-fat, high-fiber, high-fruit-and-vegetable diets will help you live longer, protecting you not only against heart disease but also against many forms of cancer.

Fruits and vegetables are particularly important for overall health and longevity. More is at stake than vitamins, which means that you won't get the same benefits simply by popping pills. Scientists haven't figured out what it is in fruits and vegetables that does the good; most likely it's a combination of factors. You may have heard the "Five a Day" slogan, which recommends five servings of fruits and vegetables each day. What most people don't know is that this slogan evolved from research indicating that we should be eating *five to nine* servings of these foods each day. Since the average American wasn't coming close to this figure, government agencies settled on promoting the more-achievable lower end of the range. Vegetable consumption is one area where more does indeed appear to be better, even up to a level that most people would consider unreasonable. French fries, incidentally, shouldn't count toward your five a day—even though, unfortunately, they're the nation's most-consumed vegetable. The oil pretty much undoes the benefits of the potatoes.

Protein. Scientific research is increasingly showing that the 50 grams or so of protein that many people have been told is all they need per day may be on the low side. The best research currently focuses on football players and other high-performance athletes, but it is beginning to look as though the average person needs about half a gram of protein per pound of body weight. If you weigh 150 pounds, that's about 50 percent higher than the standard recommendations on U.S. food labels. Just make sure you get most of your protein from heart-friendly, low-fat, low-cholesterol sources.

Salt. Conventional dietary wisdom recommends watching your salt intake to reduce the risk of developing high blood pressure. This oft-recited advice, however, has become controversial in scientific circles because many people's blood pressure is only slightly affected by the amount of salt they consume. Furthermore, running may sweat off a lot of salt, particularly in hot weather. In addition, exercise and weight loss will reduce your blood pressure, probably more effectively than the blandest low-salt diet.

Still, there's no harm in not oversalting your food. The best advice, however, is to have your blood pressure checked at least twice a year and to consult with your doctor if it's high or creeping upward.

Fueling the Serious Competitor

If you're not trying to lose weight, one of the advantages of running is that it allows you to eat more than usual. Some of this can be in the form of indulgences, such as hot fudge sundaes or chocolate truffles, although you shouldn't feel overly free to jack up your percentage of fat intake just because you're burning more of it off. But when competitive runners get above 10 or 12 miles a day, a normal diet will start producing deficiencies, particularly in complex carbohydrates and protein.

Carbohydrates are a runner's fuel. Complex carbohydrates (starches and fruit sugars) are better than simple refined sugars because they'll stick with you longer, rather than giving you a quick but transitory "sugar high."

In the past, when I was trying to maintain my racing training while traveling, I would find myself dragging for no apparent reason. I'd look back over my previous days' eating patterns and realize that I'd gotten carbohydrate depleted. A big spaghetti dinner would fix that, and the next day I'd be running my usual 17 miles, feeling just fine. Although this isn't a problem that's likely to afflict people running 20 or 30 minutes a day, it might hit you if you're trying to lose weight on the Atkins diet, the Sears diet, or one of the other popular low-carbohydrate diets. Carbohydrates are like high-octane gasoline, and you can't run happily without them.

Not eating enough carbohydrates also forces the body to look elsewhere for energy, which is why high-mileage runners sometimes look emaciated. Not only do they have no body fat, but their muscles have been cannibalized for fuel. If you eat enough carbohydrates, there's no reason for this to happen. You can run as much as 100 miles a week without losing muscle.

What the protein diets *have* discovered, however, is that most people don't get enough protein. Exercise (as discussed in chapter 2) strengthens muscles by tearing them down, then allowing them to rebuild themselves, stronger than before. Protein provides the biochemical building blocks for this rebuilding. College-level track athletes probably need three-quarters of a gram of protein per pound of body weight—well more than most of them get. Football players need a full gram. Fitness runners don't need that much, but unless you weigh less than 100 pounds, you probably need more than the amount recommended on the current food labels.

9

ACHES AND PAINS

THE RUNNING PROGRAM OUTLINED in this book is designed to minimize your chances of injury. But nobody can promise you a lifetime of pain-free running. All sports carry some injury risk; part of running *mostly* injury free is learning to recognize symptoms when they start to come on so you can nip incipient problems in the bud.

Calling these ailments "injuries" can be misleading. For many people, the term *sports injuries* draws forth images of wounded football heroes or "agony of defeat" photos of crashing skiers. Fortunately, running injuries are rarely so dramatic. Unless you sprain an ankle, break a bone, or suffer a severe muscle pull, you're unlikely to encounter significant discomfort that stays with you when you're not running. That's good news for those of us who don't like pain, but it makes it way too easy to brush off an injury as a minor complaint, unworthy of serious consideration. By trying to run through a seemingly minor problem when we shouldn't, we gradually entrench it, making the recovery slower and more difficult.

BASICS OF FIELD REPAIRS

Top athletes don't survive if they don't learn something about sports medicine. I've learned not only from my own injuries but also by swapping war stories with friends and teammates. Just by reading this chapter, you'll know more than many of your friends about the most common injuries, but you can learn more by talking to longtime runners.

Even if you never suffer a running injury, you may find great use in a basic understanding of sports medicine. The worst injury I have ever sustained had nothing to do with running: it was an ankle sprain from stepping in a hole. I knew immediately how to minimize its impact (although it still required surgery), and I knew more than most doctors about how to rehabilitate myself.

Although doctors are important for treating some types of injuries, general practitioners generally aren't your best sources of information. They may be able to help cure the ailment, but far too often they don't know what caused it. When pressed, they're too likely to shrug and say, "Well, if it hurts when you run, don't run." Like many experienced runners, I've concluded that I can give better sports medicine advice than the average medical doctor. Of course, the best of all possible worlds is to find an M.D. who's also a dedicated runner. And as the medical profession becomes increasingly aware of the benefits of regular exercise, more and more doctors will be looking for ways to keep you shipshape and moving, rather than discouraging what they know to be a healthy pursuit.

The following sections describe three things to keep in mind.

Remember RICE

RICE—an acronym for Rest, Ice, Compression, and Elevation—is the standard prescription for injured runners. The latter three are particularly important during the first 48 hours after an injury, while the body is more or less deciding how badly it's hurt. Whether your problem is a sprained ankle or an overuse injury, attentive care at this stage can substantially increase the speed of your recovery.

Rest can be anything from a complete layoff to simply slowing down a bit while the injury heals. If you stepped in a hole and your ankle looks like a purple football, obviously you need a complete layoff. With a slower-onset injury that you've caught early on, it's often OK just to try running at a reduced level initially and seeing how well that works. But be realistic; if backing off a bit isn't doing the job, bite the bullet and take a true rest now, before you have to take a longer one later. To keep fit while laid off, switch to some other sport, such as cycling, swimming, or working out on a rowing machine. As long as these forms of exercise don't hurt, you're very unlikely to be causing harm. In fact, most sports medicine experts now believe that keeping active promotes healing by pumping more blood through the injured tissue, which speeds recovery and reduces swelling. But you really have to let pain be your guide—and you have to be willing to take a total rest if that's what your body is asking for.

Ice can be applied either by applying a bag of crushed ice or by rubbing ice cubes directly against the skin. The ice bag works best with injuries that require longer application, because it's not so unpleasantly cold to the touch. Ice cubes are faster with more superficial injuries, and you can usually tolerate them for a few minutes. Don't frostbite yourself with super-chilled ice cubes applied directly from the freezer, however. Even a thin plastic bag will provide some insulation to help reduce this risk.

Sports medicine books often tell you to ice the tissue for 20 minutes at a time. Actually, all you have to do is get it good and cold. This will take longer with a deep muscle pull than with a sore Achilles tendon. But once the tissue is well chilled, you've achieved most of the benefit you're going to get; you'll spend your time more efficiently if you ice the injury again later, rather than continuing to do so now.

Compression and elevation are often done simultaneously. Whenever you get the chance, wrap the injured extremity in an elastic bandage and prop it on a footstool.

Anti-Inflammatories

Along with RICE, anti-inflammatory drugs are one of your best friends. These medications kill pain by combating the inflammation process that causes it. This means you're not just doping yourself up so you can go out and worsen your injury without knowing you're doing so. You can be fairly confident that you're OK doing anything that doesn't hurt.

Over-the-counter anti-inflammatories include aspirin, ibuprofen, and naproxen sodium. If you use aspirin, you'll probably need to take more than two at a time; many people use three. Just don't take so many that your ears ring, the first sign of aspirin overdose. With the other anti-inflammatories—which most runners today use instead of aspirin—you'll get no such overdose warning, so don't exceed the label doses without first talking to a doctor. Your chief concerns should be for your stomach and kidneys. Try not to take them on an empty stomach (taking them with milk is ideal), and keep well hydrated so the drug is nicely diluted when your kidneys excrete it in your urine. Don't use these drugs without first consulting your doctor if you have ulcers or kidney problems.

Chemically, anti-inflammatory drugs must serve two functions. One part of the molecule fights inflammation; another tracks down inflamed tissues so the inflammation fighter can be concentrated where it's needed. Which medication works for what injury isn't very predictable. If ibuprofen isn't doing the trick, try naproxen sodium or aspirin.

Aspirin, ibuprofen, and naproxen sodium are the big three of sports medicine anti-inflammatories, but new ones are being developed all the time. Any nonsteroidal anti-inflammatory (NSAID) designed for arthritis is also of potential benefit in sports medicine. Acetaminophen is in a different class of medications. It has some anti-inflammatory effect, but it's also a direct painkiller. That means that if acetaminophen dulls the pain, you can't be sure you aren't continuing to damage the injured tissue.

> **Most sports medicine experts now believe that keeping active promotes healing by pumping more blood through the injured tissue, which speeds recovery and reduces swelling.**

Stretch and Lift Weights

Injured tissue has generally been overstretched, either from prolonged overuse or a sudden pull. Your natural tendency, therefore, will to be avoid stretching it for fear of making the injury worse.

This instinct is correct, but only partly so. Reinjury is a definite risk, but total immobility can actually increase this risk. Not only will the increased blood flow from cautious motion speed the healing process (see pages 140–41), but you'll need gentle stretching to keep the injured tissue from becoming less flexible—and more injury-prone—as it heals.

Muscle, tendon, and ligament injuries form scar tissue, just as your skin does even after the most minor cuts or scrapes. This tissue will begin forming in about a week, binding the injured area back together like natural sutures. It grows randomly, however, in starburst patterns that can become inflexible knots. *Gentle* stretching encourages the scar tissue to line up in the right direction while it's still malleable. It doesn't take much stretching to achieve this: just enough to move the injured limb through its pain-free range of motion. Do it once a day, starting about a week after the injury, being careful not to stretch to anywhere near the sharp pain that signals additional injury.

Weight lifting can be beneficial for some injuries, but it requires even greater care. A pulled hamstring, for example, is going to be weak for months, even after you've returned to running. Weight lifting will greatly speed its rehabilitation, but initially you need to keep the weights very light to avoid a new pull. And you shouldn't even start lifting weights until such an injury is fairly well healed. Other injuries, such as runner's knee, respond more quickly to weight lifting because here you're not attempting to strengthen the injured tissue itself (see below). Rather, you're strengthening the surrounding muscles to eliminate the stresses that gave you the problem in the first place.

COMMON HURTS

A treatise on running injuries is beyond the scope of this book. But here are a "dirty half-dozen" or so of common injuries and tips for their treatment and prevention.

Achilles Tendonitis

Any injury whose name ends with "-itis" is an inflammation. In this case, the inflamed tissue is the *Achilles tendon,* which connects the calf muscles to the heel. There are two basic ways to injure it: overuse and overstretching. With overuse, the Achilles tendon doesn't quite have time to regenerate between workouts and gradually becomes sore; you can often find the sore spot by squeezing the tendon gently between thumb and forefinger. (Increasingly, this problem is being called Achilles "tendonosis.") Other early symptoms are pain in the tendon when you first get out of bed in the morning, pain at the start of your run, or pain when you walk, particularly in low-heeled shoes. Severe cases will produce a grating sensation when you flex the foot, but you should have done something about the problem long before it gets to that point.

Overstretching typically occurs from changing some variable in your workout too rapidly. Even world-class athletes can get Achilles tendonitis if they suddenly start using low-heeled track shoes to run high-speed laps on a track. Suddenly taking up hill running can do the same thing.

Treatment. As with any inflammation, begin with anti-inflammatories and RICE. Also, try putting a firm, ¼-inch pad into the heel of your shoes. Called *heel lifts*, these pads should be available at a modest price from any orthopedic appliance store. Use an equal amount of lift in both shoes, even if only one heel

Heel lifts.

hurts, to avoid creating an imbalance. If possible, avoid foamy *heel cushions*, which are commonly sold in drugstores. They compress under pressure, giving you less lift than you think you're getting and subjecting the back of your heel to blister-inducing rubbing. As the tendonitis abates, reduce the amount of heel lift to ⅛ inch, then to nothing. Although entrenched Achilles tendonitis can take months to resolve, most cases should be substantially improved in a couple of weeks.

Prevention. Increase workout mileage very gradually. Make sure your shoe has good heel support and that the heel is built up at least ¾ inch above the ground. Good impact cushioning in the heel may also help, although that has yet to be proven. Religiously practice the calf stretch on pages 100–101, particularly *after* each workout. Calf raises (see pages 114–15) may also help, both by increasing the calf's ability to absorb shock and by directly strengthening the Achilles tendon. If you change your workouts to include speed work (see chapter 11), hills, or even a change in running surface, phase in the change gradually, over the course of a couple of weeks, and don't simultaneously increase your mileage.

Plantar Fasciitis

The *plantar fascia* is the ligament that connects the heel bone to the toes. It has been compared to a bowstring, because it applies the tension to your foot that creates the arch. You can feel it easily, just a little to the outside of the foot's centerline.

Like any other connective tissue, the plantar fascia can become overstretched and inflamed. It too has a poor blood supply, so once it becomes inflamed, it's slow to heal, typically producing sharp, tingling pains at the point of injury, most notably at the start of your run. The tingling may be in the middle of your arch or beneath your heel, where the plantar fascia wraps around to meet the base of the Achilles tendon.

Treatment. Use RICE and anti-inflammatories, and consider massage. Massage can most easily be done with a plastic foot roller (available from an orthopedic supply store for about $15 to $20). Standing on your good leg, step on this device with your shoe off, centering it under the arch of your afflicted foot. Pressing down firmly, rock the roller on the floor so that its curved surface runs along the base of your arch, giving it a firm massage. Don't worry if this hurts. In fact, it works

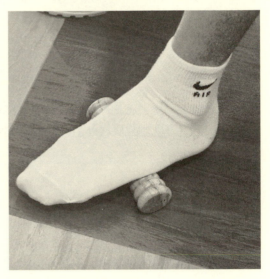

Plantar fasciitis foot roller.

best when producing as much pain as you can tolerate. Try to find a spot that feels knotted, at the point of injury. When you find it, the roller will produce a crunching sensation that you may almost be able to hear. The knot represents scar tissue forming at the site of the injury; massaging it softens the scar tissue so that it doesn't contract the ligament even further. If you don't have a foot roller, you can do the same by massaging the lump with your thumb and forefinger. In most cases, the problem should be pretty well healed in a week or two, even without a layoff. But if it's really entrenched, you may need a cortisone injection.

Prevention. Plantar fasciitis is caused by poor arch support. Imagine what would happen if you inverted a plastic bowl on the floor and then stomped down on it, hard. That's exactly what happens to your arch if there's not enough support. (Downhill skiers have a similar problem when, seeking extra control, they snap their boots so tightly that they squash the arch flat for hours on end. Many develop plantar fasciitis.) Change to more supportive shoes or invest in custom orthotics (see pages 83–84). Plantar fasciitis sufferers who buy orthotics rarely have a recurrence.

Muscle Pulls

Muscle pulls are actually muscle tears. If there's only a small amount of torn tissue, you tend to call the injury a "strain" rather than a pull and count your blessings. Any sharp, stabbing muscle pain is likely to be a pull. Severe ones can drop you in your tracks. You can also pull a tendon or the area where the muscle and tendon join. In general, the closer the pull is to the tendon, the slower it will be to heal, due to reduced blood supply.

> ## It takes about 90 to 120 minutes for your metabolism to come up to speed in the morning.

Treatment. Immediately apply ice; then rest. Even a minor pull requires a few days' layoff. Picture your muscle as a rope: the pull has nicked a few of the rope's fibers; if you continue to use it right away, there may be additional fraying. You'll also benefit from anti-inflammatories and the remainder of the RICE treatment.

Recovery to the point where you can resume running will take anything from a few days to a few weeks. Most cases will take about five to seven days, but you'll have to be careful on your first outings.

Prevention. Stretch regularly. Also, most pulls are caused by running too fast before you're adequately warmed up. Try to run at a reduced pace for about the first 25 percent of your workout. Be particularly wary of cold weather. On a cold day, it might take 10 minutes to warm up to the point you'd reach in 2 or 3 minutes on a hot day.

Elite runners are particularly wary of muscle pulls, largely because they're so preventable. For example, I modified my workout routine when I learned that body temperature drops at night, while the metabolism is reduced for sleeping. It takes about 90 to 120 minutes for it to come up to speed in the morning. So, in the days when I sometimes did hard morning runs, I never started until I'd been out of bed for at least an hour and a half.

Experienced racers are also better than beginners about warming up. In the 1980s, I spent a year living in Australia, where I sometimes ran with Robert DeCastella, one of that country's top marathoners. He was uncommonly cautious about warming up. Most elite distance runners warm up at about a seven-minute pace—about two minutes per mile slower than marathon race pace. Rob would go out at an eight-minute pace. To the rest of us, it felt like walking, but he claimed he had fewer injuries. He may have been right; it certainly didn't slow him down once he'd warmed up.

Sprains

With some injuries, familiarity breeds contempt. For example, because few of us escape childhood without twisted ankles, we don't take these injuries very seriously, painful as they are. But sprains can be more damaging and slower to heal than broken bones. When you are running, your most vulnerable point is the ankle. Any twist you can't "walk off" in a few minutes is potentially serious. Luckily, serious sprains are relatively rare among runners who stick to flat surfaces. But if your fancy also includes trail running, cross-country running, or sports like soccer or basketball, you may have to cope with these painful interruptions.

Treatment. Use RICE and anti-inflammatories. If the sprain is serious—which may be a bit hard to diagnose on your own—consider seeing a sports medicine specialist to have it evaluated and to be put on a rehabilitation program. Beware that for at least six weeks after a major sprain—and maybe much longer—you're a sitting duck for a second, worse one. Many a collegiate cross-country runner or soccer player has damaged an ankle for life by trying to get back out on it too soon. Don't be misled by basketball and football players who suffer major sprains and are back in the game within minutes. These people have had their ankles taped by experts who know how to make sure they won't sprain them again. Don't be tempted, incidentally, to tape up your own ankle and try to run on it. If you don't know what you're doing, this can cause a great deal of damage.

Prevention. Medical experts say that a badly sprained ankle never fully recovers. Minor twists recover well enough that you'll never know the difference, but major ones severely stretch the ligaments—and stretched ligaments remain stretched unless they are surgically repaired. You can compensate for even a severe sprain, however, by strengthening your ankle muscles. Try flexing and rolling your feet any time you're sitting where you don't have to wear shoes. Another exercise is to stand first on the outside edges of your feet, then on the inside edges. If you want to really strengthen your ankles, take up ice-skating. The high-top boots will prevent sprains, but the need for balance will test—and build—muscles you never knew you had.

As a former collegiate cross-country runner, I've had my share of twisted ankles and have gradually learned to give this injury a great deal of respect. Many is the time I've turned an ankle slightly, stumbled a bit, then powered on through the run—only to discover the next morning that the ankle was surprisingly swollen and discolored. Now, if I take a misstep, I slow down or stop and walk for a few minutes to see if the pain will pass. If there's even the slightest twinge after four or five minutes, I abandon the run and walk home. Pressing on, I've learned, worsens the injury substantially.

Iliotibial Band Syndrome

The *iliotibial band* is a ligament that runs along the outside of your thigh, wrapping across the point of your hip at one end and around the outside of your knee at the other. Its purpose is to keep your leg from bowing outward. Normally, it does this job unnoticed, but occasionally it becomes too tight, possibly because you've irritated it with unnatural stresses, such as from running constantly on a slanted surface or with worn-out shoes.

The tightness may lie anywhere along the length of the band, but the point of stress is almost always where the band crosses the outside of the knee. The band is supposed to pass smoothly through a notch on the knee's side, but if it's overly taught, it pops out of place with each stride, sometimes with a palpable clicking sensation. That rubs the backside of the band, inflaming it. The inflammation worsens the fit of the band in its notch, setting off a vicious cycle of increasing pain.

Treatment. Initial treatment is simply to take down the inflammation. Ice and anti-inflammatories are the best weapons, but stretching the band as described below may be all that's needed to alleviate tension enough to reverse the inflammatory spiral. DMSO (a rubbing liniment, see pages 157–58) is particularly useful for this injury, sometimes working a miracle cure in a matter of hours.

Prevention. Stretching alleviates the tightness that can cause iliotibial band problems. The figure four stretch described on pages 103–4 stretches the upper part of the band, where it passes across the hip, but it's difficult

Using a park bench to stretch the iliotibial band (right leg).

to find a suitable stretch for the band's lower portions. Your body just wasn't made to bend that way. Still, there are two stretches that work somewhat. One is to lie on your side on a low, solidly built table or bench, long enough for your whole body. Your sore leg should be on top. Now, let the sore leg droop off the side of the bench behind you, stretching its upper side. You'll probably stretch multiple small muscles, but you should also get some stretch along part of the iliotibial band.

A similarly cumbersome stretch is to stand upright, with one leg crossed behind the other, feet parallel and touching. (It's OK if the toes aren't equally far forward.) Now, using a hand for balance, bend sideways at the waist, away from the hip of the crossed-behind leg. You should feel some stretch in the hip, near the upper part of the iliotibial band.

You can also reduce iliotibial band problems by avoiding sudden changes in your workout that might stress the ligament. Such changes include running on slanted surfaces—such as crowned roads or beaches—or performing fast-paced track workouts, particularly on short, indoor tracks. Also, make sure your shoes are in good condition, and consider investing in orthotics if you tend to overpronate.

Standing itiotibial band stretch (left leg).

Stress Fractures

Stress fractures are hairline cracks brought on by workouts that cause more pounding than your bones are conditioned to handle (see pages 31–32). They start as deep, dull aches, usually in the foot or shin, but possibly anywhere up to the hip. They come on quickly but not instantaneously, taking about a week to progress from their first twinges to being debilitating enough that it may even hurt to walk.

Treatment. Despite their relatively benign sounding name, stress fractures are broken bones. They need to be diagnosed by X-ray, which means a doctor's visit is mandatory. Since the break is only a hairline crack, however, you probably won't need a cast unless you abuse the bone by continuing to try to run. And stress fractures will almost always heal completely, a major advantage over other kinds of fractures. You'll have to take a layoff, but you should be able to do any other exercise that doesn't hurt during or afterward, such as walking, biking, or swimming. Even with a bone injury, such exercises can speed recovery by helping to increase blood flow.

Prevention. Practice moderation in advancing your training (as described in chapter 2). Not only should you not increase your mileage too quickly, but neither should you turn up the intensity overnight by deciding to run faster. It also helps to use well-cushioned shoes and to run on soft surfaces as much as possible. If you decide to shift to harder surfaces, let your bones adjust by phasing in the change gradually, over the course of several weeks.

Stress fractures can also be caused by problems in your feet that give you an unnaturally jarring stride. If there is no obvious explanation—such as suddenly doubling your mileage—for your fracture, get your feet checked out by a sports medicine expert who knows something about orthotics. People who've had one stress fracture are predisposed to repetitions if they don't consult with an expert to determine the cause.

Shin Splints

Shin splints are sharp pains in the front of the shins, sometimes radiating downward to the top of the foot. You'll feel them most strongly when your foot hits the ground or if you vigorously flex it back and forth to its limits. Medical professionals debate what's really happening: some people view this as a ligament or tendon overuse injury; others see shin splints as minor stress fractures on the front surface of the shinbone. Most likely, shin splints include a gamut of injuries, with stress fractures being the worst. They also encompass a gamut of pain, ranging from mild discomfort to excruciating pain with each foot strike.

Treatment. Use ice and anti-inflammatories. Also, give your shins a respite while the condition is still mild by taking a couple of days off. Then shift your training to a softer surface for a week or so, icing the shin after each workout. Shin splints generally respond well to this treatment.

Prevention. Avoid sudden changes in running surface or workout intensity. An exercise called the "water bucket lift" sometimes helps, too. Hook the comfortably padded handle of a bucket over your toes and flex the foot, if you can do so without aggravating the injury. The goal is to strengthen the muscle that attaches to the shin so that it can absorb impact shock, rather than passing the shock on to the muscle's point of attachment to the bone. As you gain strength, add water to the bucket to increase the resistance.

Mild shin splints are a common beginner's problem that will abate as you become better conditioned. With experience, you'll also learn to recognize incipient shin splints before you have any discomfort you could truly call pain, allowing you to cut back a bit to dodge the overwork that produces them.

Runner's Knee

Runner's knee—also known as "jumper's knee," "cyclist's knee," and a host of ailments named for other sports—is an inflammation of the kneecap, although it can also come from tendonitis of the *patellar tendon*, the big tendon below the kneecap.

Runner's knee used to be called *chrondomalacia*, but this term has gone out of vogue. Technically, chrondomalacia is an uncommon arthritis-like roughening of the back of the kneecap—a problem that can occur if you run with a sore knee for so long that you begin to plow grooves into the kneecap. There's no excuse for letting a knee problem persist this long.

Runner's knee typically arises from unnatural motion in your kneecap, which normally slides up and down in a groove in the underlying bones. If for some reason the kneecap tracks sideways in its groove, runner's knee is the usual outcome.

Treatment. Use RICE and anti-inflammatories. Sometimes a gadget called a *patellar strap* will help; the leading brand is called a ChoPat strap. A pair costs about $40 from any good orthopedic supply house. The strap is simply a padded band that wraps below the knee, passing over the top of the patellar tendon, across the indentation you can feel just below the kneecap. It straps on with Velcro; pull it as tight as you can.

Prevention. Despite the fact that many people think they have "weak" knees, knee pain rarely originates in the knees. Typically, the cause lies elsewhere. The knee suffers indirectly, due to unnatural jarring or twisting

PATELLAR STRAPS AND KNEE TAPING

I've never used patellar straps, but Rick has for bicycling and hiking downhill with heavy packs. Here's what he has to say.

"Patellar straps don't immunize you from sore knees, but they can extend your pain-free range or give your knees a break while inflammation subsides. For one-time use, you can fashion a makeshift strap with first-aid tape. Wrap the tape tightly around your leg below the kneecap, just as you would a ChoPat strap. You can double the effect by wrapping another piece of tape around the thigh, about 2 inches above the kneecap. Do this with your leg extended straight, snugging

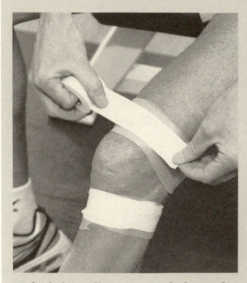 the tape tightly enough that you'd be uncomfortable squatting on your haunches, but not so tightly it digs into the back of your leg when you run. And shave your legs first or use a no-stick under-wrap, or you'll be sorry when you rip the tape off later.

"The tape works by clamping down on the tendons above and below the kneecap, shutting off the forces that tend to pull it sideways. When it works, it's like a magic switch, instantly shutting off the pain. Don't view this as a long-term cure, however. What you've done is buy time so you can track down the underlying causes."

Makeshift patellar strap made from athletic tape.

transmitted up or down the legs. One solution is to strengthen the quadriceps as shown in the photo on page 113. A weak quadriceps may not *cause* runner's knee, but a strong one helps prevent it by keeping the kneecap properly aligned in its groove.

Other potential runner's knee causes and their solutions include

- excess pronation or supination (buy motion control shoes or be fitted for orthotics)
- reaching out with your stride (review pages 89 to 91)
- running too much on slanted surfaces (avoid steeply crowned roads and find low-traffic or off-road routes where you can safely run down the center)
- running downhill (avoid courses with long, knee-pounding downgrades, and be particularly careful not to overstride on shorter descents)
- inflexibility in the hamstrings, quadriceps, or calf muscles (review the stretches in chapter 6)
- leg-length discrepancy (not everyone's legs are of equal length: if this describes you, check with your doctor or a sports trainer; the solution is to build up the shorter leg with specially designed shoes or insoles)

Solving these problems will also reduce your risk of iliotibial band problems. If runner's knee nevertheless recurs, you may suffer from *patello-femoral malalignment,* which can be caused by a problem in knee structure (correctable by surgery) but which most commonly comes from overdeveloping the outside portions of the quadriceps compared to the inner portions. This overdevelopment pulls the kneecap diagonally, irritating it with each stride. Patellar straps and taping (see the sidebar at left) will help hold the kneecap in place, but

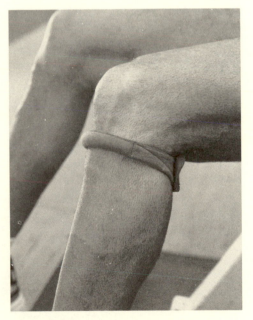

ChoPat strap in use.

you need to talk to a sports trainer about how to correct the underlying muscle imbalance.

Running rarely creates patello-femoral malalignment, but other sports do. Perhaps one in three serious cyclists, for example, suffer from it, particularly those who like to climb steep hills. Suspect patello-femoral malalignment if you have persistent knee problems and bicycle more than a few miles a week, even if bicycling itself is pain free. Even if you don't bicycle, suspect patello-femoral malalignment if you have recurrent runner's knee with no other obvious cause.

RUNNING WITH FLU AND COLDS

Many older running books (and doctors) habitually told runners never to run with an acute infection (including the common cold). When it came to colds, however, this was advice that no serious racer ever followed. If I'd taken a 10-day layoff every time I had a cold, I'd have then needed to spend the next three weeks getting back into shape for racing—an unthinkable interruption in my training.

In my racing days, therefore, I used to just gut it out, training through every such illness that came my way. But from my more recent medical reading, I've decided that the smart thing to do is to split the difference. Nowadays, when a cold first comes on, I cut back my training by about 50 percent for the first few days. But even though I'm no longer racing, I don't take a complete layoff. Medical research has shown that runners can continue to run at moderate levels without causing their colds to linger any longer than if they'd just stayed home and vegged out. In fact, my experience is that moderate running may make me feel better. I may not get well more quickly, but the workout opens my nasal passages, gets the blood moving to achy muscles, and counteracts some of the lethargy that comes with a cold. And those half-length workouts are all you need to keep in shape, even for a week or 10 days. Even performance-oriented runners won't see a noticeable setback in their training.

If you have a fever, however, you really need to take a few days off, lest you turn your flu into something worse, such as pneumonia. But with a simple cold, you don't need a total layoff—although, as a fitness runner, there's no reason not to pamper yourself if you simply don't feel up to running.

COMING BACK AFTER AN INJURY LAYOFF

Nobody likes a layoff. You start to lose fitness within a few days in a detraining process that becomes particularly noticeable after the first week. Coming back from a layoff of a month or more feels frustratingly like starting over from scratch.

Nevertheless, some injuries require rest, and if you ignore this reality, you're just lengthening the layoff they'll ultimately impose on you. You'll need at least a short layoff for any injury that gets progressively worse despite treatment, or that hobbles you sufficiently to alter your stride, raising the specter of a second, "compensation" injury from the unnatural stride mechanics.

Returning to running after a short layoff (up to about a week) is fairly easy. You may feel sluggish for a day or two, but you won't have had time to detrain significantly, and you'll bounce back quickly. Even elite competitors can be back into racing form within a couple of weeks, and you'll probably feel that you've made a 90 percent comeback in half that time.

Coming back from a longer layoff takes . . . well . . . longer. An old rule of thumb is that it takes two days for each day you were laid off, although in the latter part of that interval what you'll notice is more a lack of speed than a reduction in stamina—a greater concern for racers than for fitness runners.

You'll minimize the time needed for your comeback by finding a cross-training sport that you can do during the layoff. As little as 20 minutes of the other sport, three times a week, will greatly slow your fitness decline. The key is to pick a sport that doesn't aggravate the injury. If you're laid off with runner's knee, for example, stair climbing is probably a bad choice. But swimming might be exactly the ticket. Bicycling is also a popular way to maintain fitness during a layoff, although it's not quite as easy on the body as swimming. Let pain be your guide; if one activity hurts, try another.

One other tip: tempting as it is to try to come back full force once the injury appears to be healed, you need to start up slowly—although not as slowly as when you first started running. (I never ran more than a mile on my first two or three outings after a layoff, just to make sure I was indeed ready to go.) After that, you can build up your running time fairly quickly, as long as you don't worry about the fact that you'll be running relatively slowly. If you've been cross-training during the layoff, you'll probably be able to get back to full-duration workouts within about two weeks of a two-week layoff—and you should be feeling normal two weeks after that. Without cross-training, it may take the entire four weeks simply to build the duration back up to normal. There's nothing magic about these numbers, however, and you have to let your body be your guide. If you try to power back too quickly, not only will you feel awful, but you will set the stage for another cycle of injury, layoff, and recovery frustrations.

Back in college, I got a graphic lesson in the value of cross-training during a layoff when I was preparing for the 10,000-meter Olympic trials. My problem was iliotibial band syndrome that had progressed to the point of a painful clicking sensation with each stride. I rested and rested it, but it just wouldn't go away. While laid off from running, I also put in as much time as possible in the swimming pool in an effort to keep in shape while my knee recovered. I swam so much, in fact, that I gave myself tendonitis in my shoulder—so severely that I could barely manage to brush my teeth. It sounds comical now—me, the runner, with a swimming injury—but at the time it was depressing. Not only was I laid off from running, but now I was on the verge of not even being able to swim.

The trials were barely a month away, and I decided I'd never be ready. It was summer break, and rather than sitting around Eugene being depressed, I decided to load up my car and drive back to Boston. I'd barely made it across the Cascade Mountains, however, when my car was crunched by a pickup truck that rolled backward into me at an intersection in Bend, Oregon. My car still ran, but both headlights were smashed and the body was severely dented.

My choices were now limited to waiting in Bend for several days until my car was fixed or driving back to the university while there was still daylight. The latter was a good deal more appealing. It was an extremely fortuitous decision. While I was filling out insurance forms and getting my car repaired, someone told me about DMSO (see the following section). I tried it—and was back to running in 48 hours.

The knee had been bothering me on and off for about two months, forcing the equivalent of about a five-week layoff. There were only four weeks left until the trials, but thanks to all that swimming, I was able to get my speed back before the big event. I even made the team, placing third.

Not that making the team got me to that year's Olympics. It was 1980, shortly after the Soviet Union invaded Afghanistan. The Olympics were in Moscow, and the United States boycotted the event. But at least I'd made the team, and I learned a lot about the value of cross-training to injury recovery. I don't recommend swimming so much (and so vigorously), however, that you can barely move your arms afterward! I was desperate, and the extra swimming may have made the little bit of extra difference that got me on the team. For normal purposes, cross-training that hard isn't worth it.

A Note on DMSO

DMSO is dimethyl sulfoxide, a solvent made as a by-product of the wood-products industry. It's been used for 30 years as a rubbing liniment for superficial inflammations. I myself have used it since 1980, even appearing on national television with the medical researcher who is the substance's leading proponent. People who use it generally find that it's either completely miraculous or doesn't work at all; there doesn't seem to be much middle ground. It works best for inflammation that's close to the surface—½ inch deep at most. If you have a deep muscle pull, DMSO will probably disperse in the blood before it penetrates far enough to help.

What makes DMSO unusual is that it rapidly penetrates the skin—so rapidly that if you touch the sweaty body of another runner who's been using it, you'll find the chemical's distinct taste (sometimes compared to garlic, sometimes to clams or oysters) in your mouth only a few seconds later.

DMSO is widely regarded as safe, but it has never been approved by the U.S. Food and Drug Administration, partly because the taste makes it impossible to do the double-blind placebo-controlled studies required to prove that it works. Because of the taste, test subjects who are receiving the real stuff know it immediately, a problem that makes it impossible for scientists to sort out the substance's direct effect from its placebo effect.

Many athletes—including me—are sure of its efficacy, however. It's approved for veterinary purposes, but you don't have to go to a veterinary supplier to track it down. Many pharmacies carry it, labeled somewhat humorously as "not for human use." Chiropractors and alternative-medicine stores may also sell MSM (methylsulfonylmethane), a related chemical. Usually, MSM is taken orally in the form of capsules or dissolvable crystals, but it is also available as a lotion; DMSO is always used topically.

DMSO appears to work by increasing blood circulation to inflamed tissues, which flushes away inflammation by-products and reduces swelling—often very, very quickly. Its one drawback is that it is such a good solvent that it will also carry through the skin any other substance lurking in the vicinity.

To avoid this effect, wash your hands and the site of the injury before using DMSO, and be careful what you touch afterward. There is a story, possibly urban legend, about a man who gave himself Dutch elm disease by putting on DMSO while sitting beneath an infected tree. True or not, it's a good reminder of the need to be careful. I once made the mistake of putting on dark socks shortly after using DMSO on an Achilles tendon. Later I discovered that I'd chemically tattooed myself with dye that the DMSO had dissolved out of the socks. It took weeks for the dark spots to wear away. Now, when I see athletes incautiously slapping the stuff on in locker rooms, I point out to them they're sucking anything they've touched through their skin and into their bodies.

DMSO evaporates quickly, but I retard this evaporation by wrapping the treated surface with plastic food wrap. If it's safe for food, I figure there's probably nothing in it that DMSO will dissolve and suck into my body. When I remove the plastic after a couple of hours, I dry the skin thoroughly with a white towel before letting it touch anything that might contain DMSO-soluble chemicals.

A few athletes take advantage of the chemical's ability to draw other substances into the body by crushing up aspirin or ibuprofen tablets and mixing them with it to make a paste. The theory is that the DMSO will pull the ibuprofen into the site of the injury more effectively than taking the drug as a pill. They also assume that the DMSO and the drug will work synergistically to combat the inflammation. The downside—and it's potentially a big one—is that nobody really knows what dose to use or even if this actually works. The DMSO may simply carry the ibuprofen into the bloodstream, bypassing the stomach but not affecting the site of the injury any more strongly than swallowing the pill would. If you choose to do this, remember that you're experimenting on your body in a way the medical authorities have yet to fully investigate. Don't use any more aspirin or ibuprofen than you'd be willing to take orally.

MSM isn't as good a solvent. When used topically, it will pass through the skin easily but won't carry as many foreign substances along with it. Because I've had good success with DMSO, I've never experimented with MSM and don't know if it's equally effective.

EXPANDING YOUR HORIZONS

ONCE YOU'VE REACHED YOUR GOAL of 20- to 30-minute runs at least three days a week, you're doing as much running as you need for basic fitness. You can continue to gain benefits by increasing to 30 minutes, five times a week, but you may prefer to diversify your fitness program by adding a bike ride or two or going hiking or cross-country skiing on weekends. Running will help train you for these periodic outings, allowing you to go farther and more comfortably than you could if you were purely a weekend warrior. As an extreme example, Himalayan climbers train by doing as many lesser climbs as possible—but they also do a lot of running. For more normal people, being in shape from running will help you have a better time on an active vacation. It may even help you adjust more easily if that vacation is at high elevation in, for example, Colorado.

Many people are satisfied once they've reached this level. If that's you, there's no reason to let anyone talk you into feeling inferior, guilty, or somehow less of a runner because you don't want to run farther or faster. Enjoy your fitness, and invest your remaining free time in some other hobby.

But now that you've become a runner, there are many fun things you can do with your newfound athleticism. Maybe you're seeking a challenge; maybe you just want to diversify your workouts to avoid losing interest. The next chapter will briefly discuss a number of ways to broaden your running program. The chapters after that will then turn to the most common way of challenging yourself: racing.

As with the first part of this book, you can view it as an academic course, with a midterm and final exam. Your midterm assignment is to choose a goal that sounds like fun and work out a disciplined program to train for it. Your final—really more of a graduation exercise—is to carry out the training and revel in the accomplishment itself, whether it's a long trail run along a scenic lakeshore, a 10K race, a full marathon, or something entirely personal.

10

CHALLENGES AND ADVENTURES

RUNNING CLUBS AND TRAINING GROUPS

We've already discussed the advantages of training partners (see pages 43–44). Running clubs provide an opportunity to share the social running experience with many other people. Some groups show up to support their members at races or meet for occasional social gatherings that have nothing to do with running. If you're at all gregarious, its easy for a running club to become a centerpiece of your social life—enough so that missing the weekly outing can be disappointing.

Some clubs cater only to serious racers, but most are open to all comers. The clubs can be as informal as a noon-hour group that runs from an office complex or as tightly organized as a nonprofit organization with annual dues (usually nominal) and a monthly newsletter. Some health clubs also host group runs, typically after work or on weekends. There may be a fee in addition to your club membership fee. To locate a group in your hometown, ask the clerks at your favorite running store or check announcements in the outdoor section of the daily newspaper. Generally, to run with such a group, you need to be doing one outing a week of at least 3 miles, and you need to be able to run comfortably at a 9:30 or faster pace. It's not that slower runners aren't welcome; it's just that they won't have much company on the road. Similarly, club runs are seldom shorter than 3 miles. Most clubs, however, offer distance medleys, giving you the option, for example, of turning back anywhere along a 3- to 7-mile course.

Training groups are similar to clubs except that they are goal oriented and often offer coached workouts. Usually, all of the participants are targeting on a specific race, typically a marathon, but the diversity of speeds will be at least as high as in a running club. Because the participants are generally training for a race, their workouts are often more intense than club runs. That means it's easier to push yourself too hard and get hurt. There's not much reason to enter such a group unless you're training toward the same goal as everyone else.

TRAIL RUNNING

A gentle forest path offers a wonderful variation on your normal running routes. I've been fortunate enough to spend much of my life in Eugene and Portland, Oregon, both of which are renowned for runner-friendly park systems with broad, easy trails.

That said, trail running is more difficult than road running and carries certain obvious risks. Roots can trip you up, rocks can twist your ankles, mud can send you into a painful skidding crash, and dead leaves can hide obstacles until you find them the hard way. Add skunks, ticks, and shin-level fronds of poison oak

Running on a beautifully manicured trail is a pleasure.

or poison ivy to the threats, and you have to concede that running trails is riskier than sticking to roads or better-groomed jogging paths.

On the other hand, forest paths are cool and shady on hot summer days. They're also pleasant respites from urban hustle, and many are well enough populated by other joggers to be reasonably safe from the risk of mugging or assault. (Don't go trail running in an unfamiliar city, however, where you don't know what areas are or aren't safe.) If you choose to run trails, here are a few tips to help avoid a misstep.

- Slow down and enjoy the scenery. Trails aren't good places for speed workouts unless you're blessed with strong ankles and unusually good balance.
- Avoid rocky hiking trails. A few people do run these, but these people are greatly increasing their risk of ankle sprains.
- Be particularly careful on downgrades or sharp corners.
- If you're unsure of your footing, slow down and take short, careful strides. Walk if necessary.
- Know the human and animal risks of the area where you plan to run. Ticks carrying Lyme disease, for example, are a significant risk in New England but not a big risk in western Oregon. In some places, nobody runs in certain urban parks, even in broad daylight.
- Keep alert. The irony of trail running is that the very scenery that draws you to the trail is one of its biggest dangers. Most injuries happen when you become so absorbed in the view that you forget to watch where you're putting your feet.

If you do a lot of trail running, you might want to invest in trail shoes (see chapter 4), but for occasional outings onto relatively gentle terrain, your normal running shoes will do fine.

A gentle forest path offers a wonderful variation on your normal running routes.

CROSS-COUNTRY RUNNING

Running cross-country is like trail running without the trail. You'll probably have to enter races to take advantage of their route finding information, but if you like, you can treat these races as fun runs. Cross-country running is a lot of fun—but it's also a very easy way to twist an ankle. Not that that risk ever stopped me. In college, I was NCAA cross-country champion, and I finished second in the world championships one year and fourth another year.

The easiest cross-country routes are in parks with mowed lawns, where the chief obstacles are uneven terrain and gopher holes. The roughest courses are as close to a contact sport as you're going to find in running, but the contact comes with branches, slippery slopes, and muddy ground. Fun as it can be, I can't recommend cross-country running to beginners or anyone whose chief running goal is fitness. It's just too easy to sideline your program with an injury.

WHERE AM I?

Rick has tried a few beginner orienteering events, a European-style hill-climb, and other crossover events between hiking and cross-country running. He's an experienced backpacker, so he has the map-reading skills to keep from getting dangerously lost. Here's what he has to say:

"Off-trail route-finding events range from easy to outrageously difficult. I've participated in orienteering events held in beginner-friendly city parks or on golf courses. The sport usually involves using a map to find as many of a series of sites as possible within a set time limit, then getting back to the start before you run out of time. If you're good enough with a map you don't need to be all that speedy—and if you're speedy you don't have to be perfect with the map.

"*Hill-climbs* are also a lot of fun. The ultimate in cross-country running, hill-climbing (often called *fell running* in the U.K.) is better developed as a formal sport in Europe than in the United States. I tried it once in Scotland. The goal was to reach the top of a mountain and return by the route of my choice as quickly as possible. Uphill wasn't bad, mostly because it was so steep that even the leaders were reduced to a walk. But coming down required ankle-supporting trail shoes, good balance, and a kamikaze attitude—all of which the Scottish runners seemed to have in abundance.

"Hill-climbs can be found in some U.S. mountain states and Canadian provinces. Also catching on in some parts of North America are *scramble runs*, which follow poorly marked cross-country courses through forests, brambles, rivers, boulders, snow, and mud. They're like extreme cross-country events with the added risk of getting lost.

"If you're keen to try high-adventure running sports, you can find more information, including hundreds of race listings, in *Trail Runner* magazine."

ORIENTEERING

If you're handy with a map and compass, you may want to try orienteering. It's a lot like cross-country running, but instead of following a marked course, you have to find your way from a map. Be aware, however, that orienteering carries all the ankle-spraining risks of cross-country running, although you can minimize these by doing the course as a mixture of hiking and jogging.

Advanced orienteering events, however, are tough. The terrain can be virtually impassable, poison oak may abound, and getting lost is a real prospect. Make sure you know what you're getting into before you start, and don't be embarrassed to turn back if you start to feel in over your head.

RUNNING WITH YOUR DOG

If you're a dog owner, it's tempting to take your pooch out for a run. The exercise is as good for the dog as it is for you, and Fido's companionship may make the run more enjoyable. Most pet owners eventually give it a try.

That said, running with your dog has enough serious drawbacks that it's probably best not to do it until you've progressed beyond the beginning-runner stage—especially if your route traverses neighborhoods or parks where it's necessary to keep the dog on a leash.

The biggest problem is the risk of colliding with your pet. Unless the animal is perfectly trained to heel, the sight of a squirrel, a rabbit, or another dog can tempt it to halt suddenly or dart across in front of you, jerking you off balance or even tripping you. It's also possible to trip over an unleashed dog, but the chances are lower, simply because the dog is generally farther away from you.

Also, the dog may not accommodate well to your pace. It's not unusual for a run to start with the dog pulling you—off balance and faster than you want to run—and end with you pulling the dog, who is now ready to stop and sniff every bush or fireplug. Again, this is less of a problem with an unleashed dog under good voice control, but you may find that you spend too much of your run calling the dog away from all those canine distractions.

If running with your dog still sounds like fun, however, feel free to give it a try. Just be aware that the dog may be a complicating factor and that it may make you unpopular with walkers and other runners. Even if they're not afraid of dogs, they may not want your mutt investigating them.

The best environments for running with a dog are pet-and-owner races, which often have names like "Doggie Dash." These aren't serious races. Instead, they're great opportunities to run with people you know will appreciate your pet—and they're probably one of the most exciting activities your dog will ever get to do. Your dog will have to be leashed, though, and you'll probably need to keep that leash very short to avoid creating a hazard for other runners.

If you decide to do the local Doggie Dash or if you want to start taking your pet on training runs, remember that the dog may not be as well conditioned as you are. Dogs are natural runners, but they need to ease into it gradually, just as you did. They overheat easily, and their paws need a chance to toughen up for asphalt or concrete so they don't get cut or blistered. Also, make sure you stop occasionally to give your pet some water.

RUNNING AWAY FROM HOME

There's no reason to shelve your running workouts when you're on a business trip or vacation. In fact, trips are great opportunities to spice up your running life by taking in new routes. At the same time, running is a good way to counteract the tendency of vacationers and business travelers to gain weight from an overabundance of fine dining.

Urban Running

If you're staying downtown in a big city, ask your hotel for suggested running routes; you won't be the first to ask, and the hotel staff may even be able to give you a course map to keep you from getting lost. Or, check out library copies of *Runner's World* to see if the run-worthiness of your destination city has been profiled as part of its On the Road department. The World Wide Web is also a source of potentially useful information.

Running from your hotel is also a good way to explore the neighborhood for restaurants or shops that you might want to visit later on. When I'm in an unfamiliar city or even an unfamiliar part of a city I know fairly well, I generally end my workouts by jogging around a bit to see what's within walking distance.

For the bulk of my run, though, I prefer to get away from the stoplights, pedestrians, and crowded sidewalks of the hotel district. Waterfronts are good places for uninterrupted running, as are parks with running loops—often as long as 2 or 3 miles. Many urban parkways are also good places to run, paralleling rivers or creeks that shut off side traffic for miles on end. Sacramento, California, for example, has a 32-mile off-road bike and running path; Washington, D.C., has the 20-mile Rock Creek Parkway, and Minneapolis, Minnesota, has an off-road circuit that winds around a trio of lakes for distances ranging from 3 to 10 miles. Just be aware that you may have to share these routes with cyclists and in-line skaters.

Tourist Running

If you're vacationing at a rural retreat, it's even easier to find good running routes. You will probably be traveling by car, so if your motel or campground is badly situated, all you need to do is drive a few miles to find idyllic conditions on farm lanes, state parks, or small-town side streets.

You'll probably find that running is a good way to spot birds and wildlife you'd otherwise miss, and that it encourages you to see the sights at a pleasant, relaxed pace. Make sure you allow time to stop occasionally along the way.

If you take up tourist running, however, be careful to avoid fanaticism. As a fitness runner, you're not likely to find it much of a problem, but if you're also moving into racing, you'll find yourself tempted to do silly things out of fear of missing a workout and backsliding on your training. If your vacation is otherwise active, filled with hiking or skiing or some other sport, there's no reason to run unless you want to—and trying to force a run into such a schedule can be grueling. A week's missed training won't hurt you, especially if you're keeping up your cardiovascular fitness with some other sport.

Conversely, however, don't let a vacation layoff cause you to lose motivation for running once you return home. The less time you've been a runner, the bigger this risk is, because the vacation may tempt you back into your prerunning lifestyle. Whether you run on vacation or not doesn't matter all that much. What does matter is that you not procrastinate getting back on the jogging path afterward. Some people may need to find time for at least minimal workouts while on vacation, just so they don't lose the habit.

SIGHTSEEING AND RUNNING

Rick has perfected his own version of tourist running, in which he actually does part of his sightseeing on the run. That's not a practical way to visit museums or art galleries, but it can be a great way to tour a scenic loop in a state or national park. You can even carry a camera, if you don't mind the weight; wrap the loop around your wrist so you don't drop it.

The key to tourist running, Rick says, is to think of yourself first as being on vacation and only secondarily as doing a workout. If a scenic drive is longer than you want to run, arrange to have the nonrunners in your party meet you midway through it.

RUNNER'S HIGH

You've probably heard of it: the euphoric feeling that comes on when you feel as though you could run forever. Sometimes when it hits, your perceptions are crystal clear, etching every detail of a beautiful running course indelibly in memory. On other occasions, your mind drifts off, happily pondering anything from philosophy to baseball while your body moves on autopilot.

Not everyone experiences this sensation. Nonrunners sometimes accuse those of us who do of being addicted to pain. The theory is that when we're hurting, the body manufactures painkillers similar to opiate drugs. (It does indeed do this.) When we subject ourselves to pain, these scoffers say, we flood our bodies with these endogenous opiates and produce a biochemically induced euphoria very similar to a drug addict's high.

Those of us who've been there, however, know this is nonsense. The runner's high doesn't come on when you're hurting. I've certainly felt nothing like it in the final mile of a marathon! Rather, it comes on when you're *not* hurting—when the body is working at its smoothest. You're most apt to encounter it when you're well trained and are running in pleasant surroundings at a slow, comfortable pace. You may never encounter it at all. If you do, relish it, for it's a fleeting joy that appears of its own volition, not by an effort of your will. Just don't get so wrapped up in the joy of motion that you forget to yield to cars, step in a hole, or shatter your tranquility by running into a lamppost.

PHILOSOPHICAL RUNNING

Few sports, with the possible exceptions of mountain climbing and fly-fishing, have generated such an extensive literature as running has. Perhaps it's because, like mountain climbers, we are often asked why we do it. Whether we're running a marathon or jogging around the block, our enjoyment is equally incomprehensible to most nonrunners.

There are, of course, several answers to the "why" question. The health reasons were discussed in chapter 1. But once you've reached that basic level of fitness, you may find that running becomes something you do simply because you like to run. In the mountaineering literature, George Mallory immortalized the climber's response to this same type of question with his simple reply: "Because it's there."

> **Few sports, with the possible exceptions of mountain climbing and fly-fishing, have generated such an extensive literature as running has.**

There's an extensive running literature, much of it very well written, that attempts to answer the same question for runners. It even shows up in the magazines. *Runner's World* has much higher literary standards than comparable publications for most other sports.

To sample the running literature, the best place to start is with the writing of George Sheehan. A cardiologist who did much to promote running in the 1970s and '80s, Sheehan was also a thoughtful philosopher whose book *Running and Being* is one of the sport's premier tomes.

Other good nightstand reading includes

- *The Courage to Start* by John Bingham. A *Runner's World* columnist nicknamed "The Penguin," Bingham has written the perfect book for any beginner in need of inspiration.
- *The Lore of Running* by Timothy Noakes, Ph.D. This is the book I consult for the final word on the physiological hows and whys of racing, training, stride mechanics, nutrition, or just about anything else

that might affect performance. It's not exactly light reading, but if you want to become an expert, here's a good place to start.

- *Once a Runner* by John Parker. This is the best fictional account to date of what it's like to be a competitor digging deep to achieve one's potential.
- *The Four-Minute Mile* by Roger Bannister. For years the four-minute barrier was believed unbreakable. Now, world-class runners routinely beat 3:50. But Bannister was the first to crack 4:00—and no one has ever written more eloquently about the simple joys of running and racing.
- *Finding Their Stride* by Sally Pont. A young cross-country coach takes you inside the fall season at a little-known prep school to capture the nuances of high school running. Having coached high school runners myself, I might be a bit biased—but this is a great book.
- *Boston: A Century of Running* by Hal Higdon. Here's another recommendation on which I might be accused of bias, but others have told me that this is a must-own book for anyone interested in this venerable race. There's a chapter in it about my own 26.2-mile duel with Dick Beardsley (nicely told mostly from Dick's point of view). I was amazed by how many memories resurfaced when I read it, and by how well Hal captured the event.
- *The Runner's World Complete Book of Women's Running* by Dagny Scott and *The Complete Book of Running for Women* by Claire Kowalchik. These are the two definitive books for women runners. Both books will give you all the guidance you're looking for, from the first mile to the marathon.

11

RACE TRAINING

FOR MANY RUNNERS, racing is one of the sport's great treats. There are a lot of reasons to be drawn to it. You may simply want to see how fast you can run in an all-out effort—and it's a lot easier to motivate yourself to do so with other runners to chase than in a solo run against the clock. But performance isn't the only attraction. Racing also offers the chance to run on traffic-controlled courses, frequently in locales where you'd otherwise be

unlikely to run. Big-city races, for example, often shut down traffic so that thousands of runners can move through the urban canyons of the city center—a wonderfully energizing experience when they're free of the blare of auto horns. Other courses seek out lakeshores and farm lanes, where narrow roads normally make running unwise.

> **A typical race-training week will have four or five days of training. One will be your "long" day; another will be your speed workout.**

Racing also offers camaraderie. Partly, it's the semi-anonymous camaraderie of running with a huge group of people, followed by a huge postrace party. But if you race often enough, you'll start to meet the same people over and over, developing new racing-oriented friendships.

Racing isn't necessary for health or fitness, but it can be a lot of fun. Picking races as periodic targets is also a good way to motivate your running program.

The standard distances include

- 5 kilometers (3.1 miles)
- 5 miles
- 8 kilometers (about 40 yards short of 5 miles)
- 10 kilometers (6.2 miles)
- 15 kilometers (9.3 miles)
- 20 kilometers (12.4 miles)
- half marathon (13.1 miles)
- marathon (26.2 miles)

WHY RACE?

My reason for racing was simple: I wanted to test myself both against other runners and my own personal best times. I was blessed with the ability to win frequently, but some of my most satisfying races were ones in which other people broke the tape but I set personal records.

Now that I'm not racing competitively, I haven't entered a race since 1994. If I showed up for one, too many people would expect me to run at my former pace, and my asthma just wouldn't allow it. Like a lot of former competitors, I'm just not interested in racing under these conditions.

But for other people, it's not the race that matters so much as the sense of kinship with racing buddies who can start to feel like an extended family.

THE SOCIAL ASPECT

Rick is part of a circle of friends who often travel together to weekend races. Here's what he says:

"My friends and I race for a variety of purposes. Some of us are serious contenders for age-group medals. Some are racing for personal records, and still others are racing just for the fun of running courses distant from home. All of us, however, support one another's shared interest. Inevitably we wind up talking to other runners, some of whom eventually wind up as group members.

"If you're at all gregarious, such racing groups are easy to organize, as repeated racing makes you one of the familiar faces on the local scene. You don't have to be fast to have your own private track club."

TRAINING FOR A RACE

You don't need to do anything special to complete a 5K race. By the time you've finished the running program in chapter 2, you're already running a large portion of this race distance on your regular daily runs; all that will happen in the race is that you'll probably run a bit faster than usual, simply from the excitement. That may leave you a bit sore the next day, but it shouldn't be anything serious.

If you've worked up to 30-minute daily workouts, you're probably also ready for a 5-miler, or 8K. Depending on how fast you run your normal training distance is on the order of 2.5 to 4 miles, enough that you can probably push through to 5 miles without undue discomfort or risk of injury. Again, you might feel a bit sore after the race, but that will fade in the glow of accomplishment. Just don't try to run the race *fast*. It's unwise to push for both speed and a personal record distance in the same outing.

Preparing for a longer race requires some special training. Even a 10K is probably too big a step up over your current daily distances.

Race training involves shifting your workout load to phase in one or two longer-than-average runs. You'll still be running only three to five days a week, but you'll add mileage to at least one of these days so that you're running closer to the target race distance. If you're already running 120 to 150 minutes a week, you may be able to add this mileage simply by shortening your other workouts to compensate. Otherwise, you may need to increase your total mileage. For any race longer than a 10K, an increase in training mileage will probably be mandatory.

To simplify the discussion, we first need to shift from thinking in terms of the number of minutes you run to the number of miles. Running at your normal pace, use a track or other measured course to figure out your pace. Run at least a mile on this course to give yourself time to settle down; do more than one if you think the clock made you speed up. If you turn this pace measurement into a race against time, you're going to overestimate your starting mileage, and subsequent workouts, based on distance rather than running time, will be too hard. To calculate your weekly mileage, divide your mile time into the total number of minutes you spend running. If you're running 100 minutes a week at a 9:15 pace, for example, that means you're running a little less than 11 miles. The arithmetic needn't be too precise: plus or minus a mile is fine. Repeat this process occasionally to keep track of changes in your pace.

Other than a need to do some longer runs (see page 177), what matters isn't your daily distance; it's your weekly total. If you're running 9 miles a week, for example, it doesn't matter in terms of overall workload and injury risk whether you're doing a trio of 3-mile workouts or one 4-miler and a pair of 2½-milers. It's also important not to become too schedule bound. Back when I was running competitive marathons, I often tried to run 120 miles a week (17 miles a day), splitting the distance between morning and afternoon workouts. But if one day my morning 10-miler felt sluggish, I might hold my afternoon run to only 3 or 4 miles, making up the lost mileage the next day. Similarly, if I felt good, I might run farther, reducing the next day's mileage to compensate. The same applies to you: if you feel tired, reduce your mileage, making up for it some other day.

How many miles a week you need to run depends, of course, on the

DISTANCE COVERED IN 20-, 30-, AND 60-MINUTE WORKOUTS BY PER-MILE PACE

AVERAGE PACE (PER MILE)	DISTANCE (IN MILES) COVERED IN		
	20 MIN.	30 MIN.	60 MIN.
4:00	5.0	7.5	15.0
4:10	4.8	7.2	14.4
4:20	4.6	6.9	13.8
4:30	4.4	6.7	13.3
4:40	4.3	6.4	12.9
4:50	4.1	6.2	12.4
5:00	4.0	6.0	12.0
5:10	3.9	5.8	11.6
5:20	3.8	5.6	11.2
5:30	3.6	5.5	10.9
5:40	3.5	5.3	10.6
5:50	3.4	5.1	10.3
6:00	3.3	5.0	10.0
6:10	3.2	4.9	9.7
6:20	3.2	4.7	9.5
6:30	3.1	4.6	9.2
6:40	3.0	4.5	9.0
6:50	2.9	4.4	8.8
7:00	2.9	4.3	8.6
7:10	2.8	4.2	8.4
7:20	2.7	4.1	8.2
7:30	2.7	4.0	8.0
7:40	2.6	3.9	7.8
7:50	2.6	3.8	7.7
8:00	2.5	3.8	7.5
8:10	2.4	3.7	7.3
8:20	2.4	3.6	7.2
8:30	2.4	3.5	7.1
8:40	2.3	3.5	6.9
8:50	2.3	3.4	6.8
9:00	2.2	3.3	6.7
9:10	2.2	3.3	6.5
9:20	2.1	3.2	6.4
9:30	2.1	3.2	6.3
9:40	2.1	3.1	6.2

	DISTANCE (IN MILES) COVERED IN		
AVERAGE PACE (PER MILE)	20 MIN.	30 MIN.	60 MIN.
9:50	2.0	3.1	6.1
10:00	2.0	3.0	6.0
10:10	2.0	3.0	5.9
10:20	1.9	2.9	5.8
10:30	1.9	2.9	5.7
10:40	1.9	2.8	5.6
10:50	1.8	2.8	5.5
11:00	1.8	2.7	5.5
11:10	1.8	2.7	5.4
11:20	1.8	2.6	5.3
11:30	1.7	2.6	5.2
11:40	1.7	2.6	5.1
11:50	1.7	2.5	5.1
12:00	1.7	2.5	5.0
12:10	1.6	2.5	4.9
12:20	1.6	2.4	4.9
12:30	1.6	2.4	4.8
12:40	1.6	2.4	4.7
12:50	1.6	2.3	4.7
13:00	1.5	2.3	4.6
13:10	1.5	2.3	4.6
13:20	1.5	2.2	4.5
13:30	1.5	2.2	4.4
13:40	1.5	2.2	4.4
13:50	1.4	2.2	4.3
14:00	1.4	2.1	4.3

length of the race you're targeting. To simply survive the course without too much discomfort, all you probably need is for your weekly training to be about twice the distance of the race. And it's possible to complete a marathon in reasonable comfort on as little as 40 miles a week—about 150 percent of the race distance (see page 182). You might feel happier, however, if you're running an extra 3 to 5 miles a week above these minimums. Competitive racers run a great deal more mileage than this, but that type of training is beyond the scope of this book.

In addition to choosing your target weekly training distance, you also need to build up until you're running at least one workout at about 75 percent of the race distance. In the case of a 10K, that means you need your long run to be about 4.5 miles. For a 10-miler you need to have a track record of 7- to 8-mile trainers; marathoners like to build up to 20-mile trainers before the event (slightly longer than 75 percent of the race distance). There's no need to actually run 6.2 miles in training for a 10K if your goal is merely to finish. Race-day adrenaline will see you through the remainder of the course.

Your other training days can be whatever shorter distance you want, but at least two of the days should reach the 20- to 30-minute goal you set in part 1 of this book for overall health and fitness.

You may already be running enough weekly mileage to support a 10K race. At 10-minute miles, for example, five 30-minute workouts add up to 15 miles. Phase in your long run by increasing one day's workout by about ½ mile, reducing one or more other workouts by the same total. If that's comfortable, on each following week you can shift another ½ mile into the long workout until you've reached the 4½-mile target. Run this for two or three weeks prior to the race, and you should be ready to go. If you want to run two longer runs a week, it's OK to phase both of them in simultaneously, as long as this doesn't leave you feeling tired.

Building up your weekly mileage is riskier and should therefore be done more slowly. Furthermore, you shouldn't even start this until you've completed the first-year program presented in chapter 2. To be on the safe side, you may even want to let your mileage plateau for a few months at the week 52 level as your body continues to adjust. As with your first year's start-up training, when you begin the increase you should do so slowly so that your tendons, bones, and ligaments have a chance to keep pace with the rest of your body. As a general rule, never increase by more than about 10 percent a month. That might sound slow, but at this pace, you can double your training mileage every six months—enough to go from 30 minutes three times a week to a marathon in as little as a year.

Overtraining: Be Aware

Overtraining is part of what did me in for the 1984 Olympic marathon. It's a simple trap: with a big race looming, you feel rundown and sluggish, but instead of resting, you try to power through these doldrums—sending yourself into a downward spiral that leads either to injury or to poor performance. In my case, I had the added pressure of being favored to win even though I was coming off an injury. Although heat played a role, overtraining was a major factor in sending me to a disappointing 15th-place finish.

The symptoms of overtraining are listed on page 40. Bear these symptoms in mind as you move into racing; it's a lot easier to overtrain while preparing for a race than during your lower-key fitness-running workouts. If you're feeling rundown, convince yourself that it won't hurt to take a day or two off—or even to reduce your training for an entire week. The alternative is a lot worse. I don't know many elite athletes who wish they'd trained more intensely before major races; most admit that, like me, they'd have done better with slightly less training.

GAINING SPEED

Increased mileage and one or two longer runs a week will naturally cause you to get faster. But if you want, you can deliberately work on increasing your speed. The best way is to run on a track or a running path where distances have been marked at regular intervals—preferably every ¼ mile.

Experienced racers often do very structured track workouts, and there are entire books devoted to coaching patterns designed to elicit the best speed for any given distance. Particularly popular are "interval" workouts, where runners hammer through intense ¼-mile repeats with brief interludes for recovery.

Such workouts aren't for beginning racers. It's simply too easy to get hurt unless you have the mileage base and speed-training experience to sustain the effort—and to know when you should back off. A better choice is to do what elite racers call a *pace workout*, which trains your overall race speed, rather than helping you elicit intense all-out surges for strategic points, such as the final kick to the finish.

The key to a pace workout is to train at your desired pace for a substantial portion of the race's distance. As with any other form of training, you need to build up gradually—and as with all forms of speed training, you should do it only once a week. You shouldn't add or intensify speed workouts if you're also increasing your weekly mileage. That's a double-whammy that could easily tip you over the edge to injury.

Start your first pace workout by warming up for a mile at your usual pace. Then, speed up to your target pace, trying to hold that for a mile. Now, back off and complete your run at your normal pace. That's your speed training for the first week.

Next week, try it again, only this time hold the higher pace for a mile and a quarter. Build up the duration this way, however gradually you need to, until finally your weekly pace workouts cover 50 to 75 percent of the race distance at your desired race pace. You don't have to run continuously at the higher speed. Feel free to break up the workout with slower increments of up to a mile between the fast segments.

Don't be discouraged if your progress is slow. Building speed takes a lot more time than distance training does.

Track-Running Tip

Outdoor tracks typically come in two distances: ¼ mile and 400 meters. The difference is trivial: a 400-meter track is shorter by about 2 yards. At 8-minute miles, that comes to about half a second—not enough to worry about.

Indoor tracks are generally shorter, sometimes considerably so. Typical distances are ⅛ mile and ⅒ mile. Doing speed workouts on these tracks is difficult because they have sharp corners that are banked to a running speed that may not be yours. All those tight corners may be hard on your knees, and if you're running faster than the speed for which the track is designed, you'll be flung to the outside of each bend, where you may have to stiff-arm off the wall to keep from crashing. If you're running slower than the track's design speed, you'll have an equally frustrating tendency to fall inward at each bend, feeling like you're having to climb uphill to maintain course. In general, you're better off doing your speed workouts outdoors, abandoning them in the winter if snow blocks your usual course.

Track etiquette. The first time you run on a track, you'll probably feel a bit out of place. Tracks draw serious racers, and while you too are training for speed, you're not yet very race experienced. Unless you're a natural speedster, you may also feel slow compared to some of the others on the track. Just tell yourself you belong here as much as they do, and don't worry about these feelings of inadequacy. Few serious racers are going to object to the presence of anyone who's also engaged in a true speed workout, whatever your differences in pace.

Where you *will* upset the other runners is if you don't know how to share the track with them.

A ¼-mile track measures precisely ¼ mile only on the inside lane, so that's the lane everyone wants when running for time. The basic rule of track etiquette is that faster runners have priority. Unless you're the only one on the track, keep to the outside lanes when jogging, using the inner ones only when needed. If the track is crowded with faster runners, you may need to do your workouts on one of the outer lanes or find a day when the track's not so busy. If you do have to run on the outside, figure that each lane width of extra distance takes about 1½ to 2 seconds a lap. On the outside lane of an eight-lane track, that adds up to about 45 to 60 extra seconds a mile.

Here are some other basic rules of track etiquette.

- Don't suddenly stop or change lanes without making sure you're not cutting someone off.
- If a runner coming up from behind yells, "Track!" the runner is asking for the right-of-way. Move to the outside if there's time to do so without risk of collision.

- Don't use the track at a time when it's been reserved by a team or club unless you're a member of the club or it's a group that welcomes visitors.

Your Training Week

A typical race-training week will have four or five days of training. One will be your "long" day, where you'll be running at a gentle pace but building up to 75 percent of the target distance. Another will be your speed workout—or perhaps a second long day. Your speed workout may actually *be* a second long day if you decide to push the pace workout beyond half of the target race distance. Separate the two by easier days, or even rest days, to maximize your recovery and the rate at which you gain strength.

Some training programs recommend increasing your mileage by as much as 10 percent a week, but if you keep that up for more than a couple of weeks, you'll be playing Russian roulette with your bones and tendons. In seven weeks, you would double the number of foot strikes—something that can easily get you injured. Also, remember: don't simultaneously increase your weekly distance *and* add speed workouts. That's another form of Russian roulette.

Overtraining is a simple trap.

TRAINING FOR A MARATHON

Every year, thousands of people run their first marathons. Some have been racing for years and turn to the marathon as the next logical step in their running careers. But many are recent beginners attracted by the marathon's sense of ultimate challenge.

Although this book isn't aimed specifically at marathon training, its basic philosophy works equally well for taking on this challenge. Here too you need to progress gradually to keep from setting yourself back with an avoidable injury.

There are programs that take beginning runners and turn them into marathoners in less than a year. The trouble is that these programs are aimed at the single goal of completing a marathon, not at developing a new fitness-oriented lifestyle. Even when beginning runners survive such programs, they're apt to drop out of running shortly after the marathon.

To fit a marathon into an overall running lifestyle, it's better to make it a two-year goal. The first year is devoted to the basic program described in chapter 2, as you build up from nothing to 60 to 150 minutes of running a week. You can have the marathon in the back of your mind during this transition period, but don't start thinking seriously about it until you reach your one-year anniversary.

Now, after your first year, if you still want to do a marathon, continue building up slowly, increasing your total weekly workouts to about 250 minutes. As discussed earlier in this chapter, you need to do this very slowly—ideally, increasing by no more than 10 percent a month. Depending on how much you were running at the one-year point, that'll get you to 250 minutes in another 5 to 15 months, which is as little as 17 months after you first started running. In the later stages of this process, incidentally, you'll be more than adequately trained to try out races in the 10K to 10-mile range.

You're now up to something equivalent to 50 minutes, five times a week, running perhaps 25 to 30 miles a week, give or take a bit. At this point, you're about three months away from being able to do a reasonably comfortable marathon; if you want to join a marathon training program or team up with other marathoners at your local running club, now is the time to do it.

But you can also do it on your own. Basically, you should sneak up your mileage to about 40 to 50 miles a week—partly by adding mileage to your "long" runs—though you should only do these superlong runs once every two weeks. Initially, they'll probably be about 10 to 12 miles; by the end, they will be 18 to 20 miles. The total weekly mileage will provide the basis for your body to withstand the stress of the marathon; the once-a-week long runs are what will help you go the distance on race day.

A not unreasonable goal is to run the race on about the two-year anniversary of your entry into running—a remarkable transition from your first three-minute outings. Don't try to race the event for speed; just go out and enjoy the accomplishment of finishing. Speed training for a marathon is well beyond the scope of this book.

PURSUING ADVANCED CHALLENGES:
ULTRAMARATHONS, RELAY RACES, AND TRIATHLONS

Even for serious racers, the marathon is generally the pinnacle of their careers. But a few of us are drawn to go even further. I tackled an ultramarathon because I was looking for something I could do with the reduced lung function left to me after I'd finally stabilized my asthma. And my successful comeback at the longer distance still ranks as one of the most satisfying achievements of my career.

The term *ultramarathon* simply means anything longer than a marathon. It covers a wide range of distances. A "short" *ultra* would be 50 kilometers (31 miles), but there are also 50-milers, 100K events (62 miles) and 100-milers. A dedicated few even run 24-hour races in which the winner is the one who completes the greatest number of laps on a track. (The world record is currently 290 km/180 miles for men, 244 km/151 miles for women.) Training for an ultra is like training for a marathon, only more so. What matters is total weekly mileage and an occasional extremely long run. But it's not necessary to train at a fast pace. When I was preparing for the 54-mile Comrades Marathon, I averaged 115 miles a week, with long runs that eventually reached 40 nonstop miles. But my average training pace was only 6:45, well above the 6-minute miles I ran when training for marathons.

Needless to say, no one should run an ultramarathon until after completing several marathons. Then, those still interested should seek out training tips from fellow ultramarathoners or the few books or magazine articles that discuss this subject in detail.

Relay races are more within the reach of the average runner. Some are multiple-sport events in which each team fields, for example, a runner, a cyclist, and a kayaker. The running distance is rarely more than 10K, easily within reach of the average road racer. One of the most popular of these events is Eppie's Great Race in Sacramento, which draws thousands of participants annually. Part of the fun is forming a team and cheering one another on.

Other relay races require each runner to complete multiple legs, often over the course of 24 hours or longer. Here in the Pacific Northwest, the largest of these is the Hood to the Coast Relay, which draws 1,000 12-person teams for 195 miles from timberline on Mt. Hood to the Pacific Ocean. I had the privilege of being on the winning teams in 1993 and 1994 and found it to be about as difficult as running a half-marathon. The biggest problems were sleep deprivation and the fact that you're starting to stiffen up by the time you run your third leg (of three). But lots of intermediate runners do this event strictly for the fun of it, running 9-minute miles or slower on less than 25 miles of training a week.

Triathlons are more common and are likely to become increasingly so now that triathloning is finally a recognized Olympic sport. But they're not something this book has trained you to do unless they're extremely short. The running distance may be within your grasp, but even relatively short triathlons still require 40 kilometers (24 miles) of cycling and up to a mile of swimming. That means you have to be trained in three sports—a task that's well beyond the average fitness runner's time budget.

CHOOSING A RACE

It's hard to find any part of the country where there aren't a few races within an hour's drive. More likely, your problem will be an overabundance of choices.

The greatest difficulty in finding races comes when you're beginning. Once you've attended one race, your name and address are in a database that's apt to be sold to other race promoters. Pretty soon, rather than hunting for race applications, you'll be discarding unwanted ones that come in the mail. Also, race promoters show up at one another's postfinish parties to distribute applications to anyone who wants them.

To get started, the best approach is to stop by your favorite running store. Races are typically advertised by fliers that double as registration forms, and running stores are happy to put these where everyone can find them. The clerks can also give you tips for finding other races and will be happy to tell you how many runners to expect and which races are the best organized.

Additional information can be found in magazines, club newsletters, and on the Internet. Hundreds of events are listed by region in the back of each *Runner's World* issue, and many large running clubs print magazine-grade publications that combine finishing results from the previous month's races with classified ads or even registration forms for upcoming events (look for these regional magazines in your local running store). Newspaper outdoor pages are also good sources of race information, although they tend to publish only the upcoming weekend's events rather than extended calendars.

Finding information on the Internet is more difficult because there's no comprehensive, nationwide racing site. You wouldn't want one, anyway, because there's no reason to wade through dozens of race announcements from Georgia if you're looking for something to do next weekend in northern California. Ask your running store for the Web addresses of organizations serving your city or region, or visit the Web sites of specific races (the addresses are often printed on the registration form) and look for links to regional organizations or race hotlines.

GOING THE EXTRA DISTANCES

One needn't be a world-class runner to take on the challenges of longer races.

Rick once did a 24-hour relay, in which ten-member teams ran in rotation on 1-mile legs. He compares this to a half-marathon in difficulty, noting that it depends somewhat on how close to your maximum speed you choose to run each leg. Relay races are nowhere nearly as popular as standard road races, but there are probably a few each year within weekending distance of your home.

Rick has also done several triathlons, including a pair of Hawaii Ironman imitations (2.4 miles of swimming and 112 miles of cycling, followed by a full marathon). Training for middle-of-the-pack finishes, he put in the normal marathon training plus 200 miles of cycling a week and what he calls "just enough swimming so I wouldn't drown." It was still a 20-hour-a-week job. The races themselves took him anywhere from 2 to 13 hours, depending on length.

Registration fees range from about $12 to $25. People who run without paying are called "bandits" and aren't appreciated. Unregistered runners are particularly unappreciated if they cross the finish line, thereby triggering the timing clocks but giving the computers no name with which to match up their times. If you run unregistered, you're stealing from the race. Bandits who cross the finish line mess up the standings for everyone else. Putting on races costs money (one of the biggest expenditures is for portable toilets, which you'll probably appreciate), takes a lot of staff time, and generally produces a pretty good bargain for a rather nominal fee. If you want to save money, pick races where you're given a choice of a discounted entry fee without the souvenir T-shirt, and sign up well in advance, when fees are relatively low, rather than paying a premium for race-day registration.

Gimmick Races

Race promoters are always seeking ways to differentiate their races from everyone else's. Some simply hunt out fast, flat courses. Others go for scenery or hill-climbing challenges (if you don't like hills, beware of courses that circle lakes; they're not always as flat as you might expect). Others seek a gimmick to draw runners looking for something unusual. Such races take many forms, such as running through tunnels, crossing major bridges, or shutting down freeway viaducts.

There are also "predicted time" runs (no watches permitted) in which the participants guess how long they will take to finish and the winner is the one who guesses the closest. You don't have to be speedy to win, but you do have to have enough running experience to have a good estimate of your pace.

One of the more innovative races to hit my town recently was a "beat the bridge" run in which the race finished just after crossing a drawbridge that was set to be raised at a specified time. People could start running as far in advance as they wanted, but only those who made it to the bridge in time got the souvenir T-shirt. For some, it was an exercise in brinkmanship—seeing how close they could come to disaster while still reaching the bridge on time—but most people were far more conservative.

Successful gimmick runs other than predicted time runs tend to be large-scale events. Small races simply don't have the clout to persuade the civil authorities to rearrange traffic patterns to accommodate them. Expect at least 1,000 runners at most such races.

12

RACE DAY

New York City, 1981.

WHETHER IT'S A 5K FUN run or something longer, you're apt to greet your first race with a mix of anticipation and trepidation. Everyone else seems to know exactly what to do, and unlike the party atmosphere you'll discover after the big event, beforehand many runners are nervous and uncommunicative. They'll answer basic questions like "Where's the registration table?" or "Are those the only toilets?" but they're not likely to want to take beginners by the hand and lead them through the process. Larger races (those with more than 1,000 runners) are particularly intimidating, yet these are exactly the type of megaevents that hold the greatest appeal to beginners. Small races can get lonely midway through the course, when there are only a few other runners in sight. In large races, the collective adrenaline of an enor-

187

mous mob of runners is almost palpable and is a major part of their attraction. A few races draw more than 30,000 people! USA Track & Field's Web site lists the hundred largest races in the United States. Other countries also sometimes host enormous races, but data on these are harder to find.

Luckily, it's easy to learn race-day basics so that you're confident of arriving at the starting line unflustered, ready to concentrate on running. Let's walk through a typical race day, from the evening before through the postfinish celebration.

> **Experienced runners can sometimes feel the performance-dampening effects of a single drink the morning after.**

PRERACE PREPARATIONS

Obviously, the night before a race isn't a great time to take in a midnight movie. Most races start early in the morning, so you want to get to bed early. Hitting a bar is also a bad idea. Just as airline pilots aren't allowed to fly within ten hours of taking a drink, experienced runners can sometimes feel the performance-dampening effects of a single drink the morning after. One beer won't have much impact, but two may leave you feeling sluggish. Alcohol also dehydrates you, so be particularly careful about drinking (or at least keeping hydrated) on the night before a warm-weather race.

The degree to which you want to limit your prerace activities depends on how much you care about how well you run during the race. That late-night movie or second beer won't keep you from crossing the finish line, but it may make the race feel harder.

The prerace dinner is a major ritual among many racers who talk of the importance of "carbohydrate loading" with high-starch, low-fat dinners such as pasta and potatoes. Do this if you want, but it's not very important unless you expect to be running more than about 75 minutes. Carbohydrates are good because they're easy to digest, but what really matters is to avoid eating a heavy meal that's still with you in the morning. Also important is to eat foods that you're used to; experiments can lead to abdominal woes under the stress of racing.

You may wonder what to eat for breakfast the morning of the race. The answer is simple: nothing, unless you eat it at least three hours before the start—and a meal even four hours before should be fairly light. Eating any closer to race time is courting a side stitch. Unless you have unusual blood sugar problems, you'll have ample reserves from that prerace dinner to see you through. If you absolutely *must* eat breakfast closer than three hours to the event, keep it as light as possible: a glass of orange juice, a banana, or both probably won't do you too much harm two hours before the race. Or, you can mix up a drink from one of the many carbohydrate energy powders now on the market. These athletic foods are designed to clear your digestive tract quickly and are generally safe if consumed at least 45 minutes before the race.

You can also have your morning cup of tea or coffee. These no-calorie beverages don't linger in your digestive tract any longer than water, and you certainly don't want to complicate your race with a debilitating caffeine-withdrawal headache. Even people who don't normally drink coffee might consider having a couple of cups the morning of the race. Caffeine has been proven to give you extra energy—so much so, in fact, that caffeine pills (about the equivalent of eight cups of coffee) have been banned as illegal drugs in top-level competition. The only downside is that caffeine is a diuretic, forcing you to urinate out not only the liquid in your coffee but additional water as well. Compensate by drinking extra water before you run, and resign yourself to a couple of last-minute trips through the toilet line.

The vast majority of races are held in the morning, seldom later than 10 A.M., and generally earlier. A few, however, are held at dusk or even on special midnights, such as New Year's Eve. Unlike morning races, it's hard to time your eating to run such events on an empty stomach. Treat them as fun runs, even if you normally race more seriously, and try to schedule your day so you haven't eaten a major meal within four hours of the start. If that means skipping dinner, try a prerace banana or candy bar a couple of hours before the event—just enough to preclude hunger.

Prerace Eating in a Nutshell

Here's my checklist for eating before a short to midlength race (anything up to about a half-marathon).

- Go a little stronger on carbohydrates the day or two beforehand, just to make sure you've topped off your fuel tank.
- If you eat breakfast, do so at least three—preferably four—hours before the race and go extremely light on the fat and protein. I used to eat at 6 A.M. if the race started at 10 A.M. For starts earlier than about 9 A.M., I preferred not to interrupt my sleep, so I skipped breakfast.
- Caffeine is good, not only to wake you up for an early start but also to give you extra energy.

For longer races, the checklist is somewhat different.

- Make sure you're on a carbohydrate upswing before the race start, eating high-carbohydrate meals such as that runner's standby, spaghetti.
- Breakfast is more important. For marathons, where I wanted breakfast at all costs, I'd get up well before dawn, eat, and go back to bed. Most people won't want to do this, however, because it can be difficult to get back to sleep. Many middle-of-the-pack runners skip breakfast even for marathons or snag a banana or a carbohydrate drink a couple of hours beforehand. But I had a stack of pancakes five hours before I started what became my Boston Marathon win.

FROM YOUR DOOR TO REGISTRATION

Dress for the race at home; very few races provide changing rooms. If the morning is chilly, pull a jacket and loose-fitting sweat pants over your running attire. Many races will have places to check this gear at the start, typically by putting it in a plastic bag with your registration number written on the outside. Otherwise, you can leave it in your car or trust the honesty of your fellow runners by tossing a gym bag in an out-of-the-way corner.

Leave for the race well ahead of the start. If it's a long drive to the race, you might consider going to the host city the night before, using the race as an excuse for a weekend excursion. Remember that you not only have to find the start, but you may also encounter a traffic jam of other runners or a shortage of convenient parking places. You also have to deal with registration, a process that generates lines at some large races. Most runners are last-minute people; if you arrive at the start an hour in advance, you'll

CAR KEYS, TOILET LINES, AND GYM BAGS

As an elite runner, I always had a coach or could ask the race officials to help me with many of the logistical problems faced by most runners. I also had access to a private bathroom close to the start. Rick, however, has run scores of races at which he has had to fend for himself. Here are his suggestions on several important details.

"If everyone you know is competing in the race and you don't have a spouse or friend attending the race with you as a cheering section, you're going to have problems figuring out what to do with some of the things you've brought to the race. I never worry about leaving my warm-ups in my car or simply tossing my gym bag in a corner (if there's a building available for the purpose), as long as they aren't the latest statement in running fashion. If they are expensive, I prefer to check them with the race officials.

"My keys and wallet are a different matter—these I'd rather not even entrust to the race officials in the event a mix-up results in someone else getting both my keys and my address. On training runs, I carry them in a small fanny pack (see page 81), but in races, I don't want even that small amount of excess mass.

"I solve this home security concern by storing my keys and wallet separately. I hide my wallet in my car before I arrive at the race. Then I leave the keys in my checked clothing or in my gym bag (if it's not in the car), on the theory that, if anybody steals the bag, they won't know which car the keys belong to. In the rare case there's nowhere to stash my warm-up clothes, I carry my keys in a fanny pack. Other runners use magnetic key cases to secure their keys to hidden parts of their cars.

"No one wants to take a toilet break in the middle of a race. If you anticipate a problem, try getting up earlier than you need to. Some people find that drinking a hot beverage—tea, coffee, or simply hot water—shortly after they wake up will stimulate bowel action. Others find that simple prerace nervousness does the job.

"Once you arrive at the race start, however, be prepared for long lines at the toilets. All told, it's another good reason for arriving at the start well ahead of the race."

probably have easy parking, no crowds, and plenty of time to get registered without panic.

Most races use a combination of mail-in or Internet preregistration and on-site race-day registration. Registering in advance saves money, but you still have to arrive early enough to pick up your registration packet at the start, unless the race offers packet pickup at a convenient location a day or two beforehand. On-site registration involves filling out the registration form and paying your entry fee. All races accept checks, sometimes more readily than cash; don't forget to bring one. You may have the option of buying a T-shirt, but many races make only enough shirts for preregistered runners. Most have separate check-in lines for on-site registration and for preregistered packet pickup. Read the signs so you don't waste time standing in the wrong line.

Your registration packet may include a number of items, ranging from meal coupons to advertising fliers. The most important is your race number, which is printed on a piece of waterproof, tear-resistant paper. Attach it to the front of your shirt or running shorts with safety pins. If the packet doesn't contain pins, there will be a bin of them somewhere in the vicinity of the registration table. Many race numbers have tear-away segments at the bottom. *Do not* attach the number to your clothing in a way that makes these segments difficult to remove. When you finish, race officials may be planning to use the tear-aways to keep track of the finishing order of the racers. There won't be time to unpin the number from your clothing to free up the tear-away segment.

Now, all you have to do is visit the bathrooms and stretch out while awaiting the start. Try to do the bathroom visit as early as possible, as lines tend to grow with the approach of the race's starting time.

THE START

A few minutes before the race begins, race officials will start herding runners to the starting line. At the same time, the top competitors and others who are seriously racing the clock will be taking short warm-up jogs. There's no need to join them unless you too are racing for time and aren't worried about being overtaxed by the extra warm-up distance. When fun running, you can use the first few minutes of the race as a warm-up, just as you do on your training runs. Now, however, is a good time to continue stretching gently and to make sure your shoes are properly tied.

At the start, you'll be directed to line up according to your expected pace—faster runners in front, slower behind. Sometimes, particularly at large races, there will be signs directing you where to stand: 8:00 milers here, 10:00 milers there, and so forth. Pick your spot based on the average speed you realistically expect to run over the entire racecourse. If there are no signs, you will have to guess. Typically, the middle of the pack in a

5-miler is about a 9:00 pace. Three-quarters of the way forward is about a 7:30 pace, and three-quarters of the way back is a 10:00 pace—although in some races much of the back of the pack is reserved for walkers, who'll be going a lot slower than that. Longer races will have fewer really fast runners. Feel free to ask other runners their expected paces, and adjust your position accordingly.

If it's your first race, you'll have no idea how you'll react to the excitement. Line up according to your training pace; you'll probably run faster

MIDDLE-OF-THE-PACK SAFETY AND ETIQUETTE

I've never experienced a large race from anywhere but the front of the pack, but Rick has. Read his advice for middle-of-the-pack runners here and in other sidebars throughout this chapter.

"Be prepared for the inevitable runners who lie about their expected paces in order to queue up near the front of the pack. Such runners block the course and slow down everyone else, even causing dangerous situations. More times than I can count, running 6-minute miles, I've nearly run down runners who somehow managed to stay ahead of me for the first half a mile but then struggled along at a slow jog. Rudeness aside, if you do this, the dispiriting result is that hundreds of runners are going to pass you—some silently cursing—until eventually you drop back to your own speed group. It's a lot more fun to run the whole distance with evenly matched companions."

than that, but in a fun run it's better to err by starting too far back than too far forward. That way you'll be passing people rather than being continually passed.

The start will be preceded by last-minute announcements from the race officials. Make sure you listen; they might be warnings about obstacles along the course. The start itself won't be the "ready, set, *go!*" you may have anticipated. Starter's pistols are also obsolete. Most likely, you'll get repeated warnings such as "one minute until the start," then the starter will sound a blast from an air horn.

Once you get started, resist the temptation to blaze out at a selfdestructive speed. Most beginning racers, deceived by running in a crowd overcome by excitement, run the first mile at a pace far faster than they can sustain. You'll feel fresher later on if you don't overdo the start.

Beginning at the 1-mile mark, and every mile thereafter, you may find race officials calling out *split times*. Often referred to simply as *splits* in racer slang, these are nothing more than clock readings partway through the race. They're particularly important to competitive racers but can help anyone

A NOTE ON SPLIT TIMES

In the major races that draw elite athletes, course markers and split times are usually accurate. This may not be the case, though, in small or low-budget events. Here's Rick:

"During the race, I always pay attention to my split times, but I don't necessarily trust their accuracy. On flat courses, I generally run an extremely even pace and am immediately suspicious if the split times say substantially otherwise. If one mile, for example, is 30 seconds slower than expected and the next is 30 seconds faster, I figure that somebody put the mile marker in the wrong place. I've also been in races where the split times were very consistent—and way off from any pace I could possibly have been running. Use split times as guidelines to how you're doing, but also condition yourself to read the pace signals your body gives. With practice, you'll learn to tell the difference between a pace that will exhaust you in a mile and one you can sustain over the race course."

maintain a steady pace—presuming, of course, you aren't too tired to do the arithmetic needed to figure out your speed from one mile to another.

Some races don't bother to station officials with stopwatches at each mile; instead they just mark the miles and let you keep track of the time on your own. If you don't have a watch, it's a bit rude to ask other runners to tell you what their watches say; they may be saving breath—and concentration—for other purposes.

Noncontact Sport?

As an elite runner, my concern at race starts was to avoid being tripped up by people seeking their moment of glory by running, however briefly, with the front pack. Because of this risk, leading competitors have to jump out instantly upon hearing the starting horn—not quite as explosively as a sprinter off the blocks, but close enough. It's not that a couple of tenths of a second are likely to matter in a long race (although I did win the 1982 Boston

Marathon by only 1.5 seconds). But in races like the New York City Marathon, with 35,000 other runners breathing down your neck, getting trampled is a real fear. The best defense for most elite runners is to sprint out at full speed for the first few hundred yards—even if that wastes energy—until they've opened up a large enough gap on the main body of the pack that they can drop back to their normal race pace. As a former track runner, this was never a big problem for me, but I always had to start out with my elbows wide to keep people from intruding on my space. And I've known top competitors to be seriously jostled by glory-hounding rabbits.

Frantic scrambles at the start are particularly tough on the top women in races that don't offer separate male and female starting lines. The elite women have a right to line up in front, but there may be dozens or hundreds of slightly faster men behind them, threatening to step on their heels.

MORE ON SAFETY AND ETIQUETTE

As a front runner, I always had a clear field ahead of me from the outset. I wasn't completely free of the crowd (see above), but Rick's experiences with mass starts are close to what you're likely to encounter. Here's what he's learned:

"One of the ironies of being in the middle of the pack in a large race is that everyone's keyed up for the start, then the horn sounds . . . and not much happens. Everyone around you surges a step forward, then discovers there's nowhere to go until the pack ahead begins to move. It's somewhat comical: the race has begun, the elite runners are already out there somewhere, streaking ahead, but everyone in your vicinity is standing still. Don't worry; you'll be running soon enough. Only the largest races will keep you standing more than a few seconds. That will be followed by a slow walk that gradually evolves into a jog. It may be several minutes before the pack thins enough to give you running room to stretch into your normal stride.

"In really large races with congested starts, getting to the true starting line can take more than a minute—in San Francisco's famous Bay to Breakers run, with 70,000 runners, it can be 20 or 30 minutes until the back of the pack gets moving. Very few runners care about time in races like this. Everyone else does them just to be part of that sea of moving humanity.

"If you're running a larger race with the goal of posting a good time, don't worry about the official clock. Turn on your own watch when you actually reach the start line—that 'real' starting time is what matters for your purposes."

MORE SAFETY AND ETIQUETTE

Courtesy to fellow runners isn't merely a starting-line duty. As long as you're running in a pack, courtesy should extend throughout the race. Elite runners have to be careful not to step on each other's heels; here's Rick's experience running with packs that can number in the thousands.

"In a large pack of other runners, be careful not to make sudden changes in speed, particularly in the first mile or so. If your shoe comes untied, carefully move to the side, well off the course, before stopping to tie it. If you drop something, consider it gone; whatever you do, don't stop abruptly, trying to go back. If you absolutely must retrieve it, move to the side and wait for the pack to thin. Similarly, don't dodge sideways to avoid potholes, slower runners, or other obstacles without first checking over your shoulder to make sure you're not cutting someone off.

"For the same safety reasons, running with your dog is prohibited in most races. Even if it isn't, it's bad etiquette except in special pet-and-owner races unless you line up in back and stay there, where you can't possibly trip someone with the leash.

"Some people feel a need to spit every few hundred yards. If that's you, remember that the people behind you won't welcome your sputum. Move to the side and aim where you won't hit another runner or a spectator."

IMPORTANCE OF STAYING HYDRATED

Generally, *aid stations* are provided every few miles. These are simply water stops, staffed with volunteers eager to hand out cups of liquid to passing runners. In a 5K race, there's not much reason to drink before the finish. But in anything longer, you shouldn't pass up the aid stations, particularly if it's hot. When you approach one, move to the side of the course nearest the water (in some races, it will be on both sides), leaving the center free for runners who choose not to drink. Slow down as much as necessary to grab one or more cups, but don't stop right at the table, where you're blocking other people's access. Get out of the way, then drink, slowing to a walk, if necessary. When you're done with the cup, the aid station personnel—who are volunteers, not paid employees—will bless you if you at least toss it in the general direction of a trash can (if one is provided), or

drop it as soon as possible after the aid station so they don't have to retrieve cups from half a mile down the course. Many runners pour water
over their heads rather than drinking it, but if you can get it down, the
water will do you more good in you than on you.

Sports Drinks. Some races give you a choice of water or sports drinks.
Pick water unless you've practiced drinking sports drinks midway through
training runs and are sure the one offered by the race is mixed to the right
proportion. These drinks contain sugar, and if there's too much of it, the
drinks will draw water into your gut by osmosis. This not only delays the
process of hydrating yourself, but it can have unpleasant gastric conse-
quences. Some runners have suffered sudden diarrhea. These drinks (particularly the bottled ones) have this extra sugar to make them more
palatable as snack beverages for nonathletic consumers. Gatorade, for example, needs to be diluted by a factor of two for drinking on the run.

Sports drinks are useful in long races where you've dipped deeply into
your energy reserves, but for any race that takes less than an hour, you'll
never get depleted enough for them to have much effect—unless you've
done something silly like not eaten much the day before. For this reason,
relatively few short races provide anything other than water. If they do,
there's no reason not to accept it. Just make sure you know how the contents of that cup were prepared before you drink it. And be aware that the
people at the aid station may not know the answer.

Two Cautionary Tales

My greatest personal lesson in the value of hydration came in the 1979
Falmouth Road Race. Having taken second the year before as a college
freshman, I was favored to win, but it was muggy and hot (about 85°F),
and heat was always my nemesis.

I first started to get in trouble the night before, when a television crew
filmed me and the other invited runners at dinner. It took about three
hours, sweating all the time under bright lights. I probably started to become dehydrated then, but I failed to realize it and didn't drink much before I went to bed. The next morning, I compounded the error by not
drinking much before the start because I viewed 7.1 miles as a short race.

Dehydration is insidious. Walkers can faint and collapse; so can construction workers on hot roofs. Even a 7.1-mile race, I learned, can be
enough to tip you over the edge if it's hot, you haven't been drinking

enough, and you're pushing yourself to the maximum. Since then, I've even seen milers overheat and collapse, and the mile is a race that takes only about four minutes. Presumably, they too had been dehydrated before they started.

The last thing I remember at Falmouth was watching Bill Rodgers pulling away from me, about a mile from the finish. It was dreamlike—there went Bill, floating away, and I wasn't able to summon the energy to go after him. In the next mile I faded from second place to tenth, but I have no memory of being passed by anyone.

I do remember lying on a gurney at the finish. The doctor was saying I had a temperature of 108°F, and I knew exactly what that meant: brain damage or worse if they didn't get it under control immediately. I thought I was going to die. So did my father, who had a priest administer last rites.

The medical crew at the finish line was well prepared and saved me by packing me in ice. That brought my body temperature down so quickly that after an hour and a half of being intravenously rehydrated in a hospital, I was able to go home, luckily no worse for wear. But I learned more than I would have liked about the dangers of hot-weather dehydration. Anytime the temperature is above 75°F, you need to drink more water than usual, particularly if it's humid. When the temperature is above 80°F, you need to be fanatical about it.

A shift from hot to cold can also produce a runaway change in your core body temperature. This happened to me in the 1982 Boston Marathon, after I outkicked Dick Beardsley over the last mile to the finish on a 72°F day. That's not dangerously hot, but I'd again become severely dehydrated, having taken only a few mouthfuls of water during the race. Afterward, the officials herded the early finishers into a cool, damp underground garage.

There's a medically well-known phenomenon that afflicts people rescued from plunges into cold water. When chilled, the body protects itself by shutting down blood flow to the skin and extremities. That's why your feet and hands get cold. But the shutdown isn't complete. If a dangerously chilled person is warmed up too *slowly*, blood circulating to the cool exterior continues to chill the core. It's a delayed effect; at first, rescued people appear to be recovering nicely, then after about 45 minutes they can go into shock and die.

Something similar happened to me. Running had opened all of the capillaries to my muscles and skin. Now, in that cool garage, those capillaries acted as a refrigerator, cooling me faster than my body's temperature regulation system could react. Being sweaty didn't help. I now know that it's important, after a run, to get into a warm environment quickly—especially for low-body-fat racers, who don't have much insulation under the best of conditions. At Boston, I started to shiver uncontrollably, and the medics found that my body temperature had dropped to 87°F before they wrapped me in blankets and began administering intravenous fluids 30 minutes after the race. It was embarrassing to have medical problems twice in such close succession, but this one was much milder and I recovered quickly.

MORE SAFETY AND ETIQUETTE

Elite racers typically get motorcycle escorts to help clear the route. You won't. Here's Rick on middle-of-the-pack road hazards:

"Large races generally have 'closed' courses on which cars are excluded from one or more lanes of traffic, and police guard the intersections. Often, the closed lanes are marked by orange traffic-control cones. Don't venture into lanes that are open to traffic, and keep alert for cars that occasionally find their ways even onto a closed course. Be doubly alert at railroad crossings. Trains have been known to stop races, sometimes cutting through the middle of the pack. If that happens, don't even think of trying to dive between cars, no matter how slowly the train is moving.

"Other hazards are traffic islands and those white knobs sometimes used as lane dividers. If you're not paying attention, the pack can suddenly divide in front of you, like the Red Sea before Moses, as other runners go right and left, leaving you only a step or two from disaster. Some runners refer to the biggest of these knobs as 'elephant turds,' but even if they're only canine sized, they can twist an ankle.

"Elsewhere along the course, kids may be out by the street with garden hoses, offering to cool down passing runners. Most runners appreciate it, but I don't like the shock of the cold water. If you're like me and don't want to be sprayed, steer to the far side of the course and make your preference known. If you do choose to be sprayed, try to keep your shoes dry to avoid the risk of blisters. 'Not the feet!' I call out if a spraying seems unavoidable or if it's so hot that even I want to be hosed down. Not that the kids with garden hoses always listen."

Drinking on the Fly

Drinking on the run is a skill that takes practice. Prior to my first marathon, my coach set up a table next to the university track so I could practice snagging a beverage and drinking on the way by. Don't try to slam the whole cup in one big gulp. You'll probably gag and spray it back out like a scene from a bad movie. Instead, take as many small sips as needed, carrying the cup with you until you've finished. That way you never have to try to hold your breath while you swallow, one of the things that gets you in trouble. Even with small sips, though, it takes practice to get the timing right. Eventually, you can learn to sip an 8-ounce cup of water surprisingly quickly. But if you're having trouble, it's better to just cut your pace however much is necessary to get that drink inside you. It'll pay dividends later.

Elite runners often bring their own water bottles stocked with their favorite drinks, leaving them at special tables along the course. I seldom bothered. I just drank whatever the race provided—water or Gatorade—as long as the Gatorade was properly diluted.

During the race, you're going to be losing water faster than your body can replenish it. That means that in hot weather or in longer races, it's important to keep drinking throughout the course. But because your stomach can only absorb two to four cups of water an hour, there's no reason to drink more. It will just slosh around uncomfortably, waiting to give you a side stitch.

This is why people like me, who sweat a lot, are doomed in hot-weather races. In the 1984 Olympic Marathon, on an 80°F day in Los Angeles, I drank a quart of water within two minutes of the start and drank more during the race than anyone else I knew of, but I still sweated off 12 pounds before the race was over. Given what I was drinking, that meant I was sweating off something better than three quarts an hour—far faster than my body could rehydrate.

AT THE FINISH

The finish line is often a scene of organized confusion. In small races, you'll just run across it and stop. In larger ones, you'll be directed into chutes marked by colored ribbons or other crowd-control barriers. Sometimes there are separate chutes for men and women, sometimes not. Be attentive,

BAR-CODING RUNNERS

Some races offer electronic timing, which operates from a computer chip that hooks into your shoelaces. It's not quite a bar code, but it functions about the same way. When you cross the start line, you step on an electronic mat that recognizes your chip and records the precise moment you got there. After the race, you step onto a similar mat, which scans and clocks your arrival at the finish. A laptop computer tabulates the results, providing an instant printout of race standings. Don't take the chip home as a souvenir; the finish-line officials reuse them for the next race and thus keep entrance fees down.

Chip-based timing sounds like the wave of the future, but it isn't without drawbacks. It does provide quick, accurate results and greatly reduces finish-line congestion. It also reduces the tendency of runners to cheat forward at the start, since they know their times will be calculated according to when they actually reach the line, regardless of how long it takes their part of the pack to get moving. It's possible to be caught in the toilet line at the start of the race and still run a good time, coming out of the back of the pack. But electronic timing makes tactics difficult for runners chasing high places in the standings because they and their age-group competitors don't all have the same starting time. That means you can pass people in the final mile and still lose to them due to the difference in start times—an aggravating discovery.

Nevertheless, electronics will continue to play a big role in race timing. The same shoe chips could be used in races with conventional simultaneous starts. And, bar-code scanners are an obvious tool for rapidly processing runners in the chutes to obtain quick, computer-generated standings.

Even more interesting is the use of shoe chips to keep track of split times. A few races place sensor mats at each mile along the course, allowing runners to get printouts of their splits or view them on the World Wide Web after the event. This gives you an accurate record without the burden of trying to memorize your splits or risk pushing the wrong button when you try to store them in a sports-watch memory. If the chip readouts are fed directly into a Web site, friends and family can even log on from home to track your real-time progress. It's like converting your family into a virtual-reality cheering squad—even if you'll not hear the cheers until later!

and go where you're directed. And don't halt the moment you cross the finish line. Jog a few paces; then move through the chute at as brisk a walk as the person ahead of you, so there's room for the people behind you.

Don't pass other racers in the chute or let them pass you. The purpose of the chute is to keep finishers in order long enough for race officials to pull the tear-away tags off their race numbers or otherwise record their order. It seldom takes more than a few seconds, but if you get out of sequence, you mess up the race results not only for yourself but for everyone who finished near you.

Now, you're ready to relax. Walk a bit to cool down; then head for the refreshment table. Water and bananas are de rigueur; you may also find oranges, bagels, or energy or fruit bars provided as a product promotion. Remember that these refreshments are intended as a snack, not a full meal. Don't chow down more than your share before everyone else has had a chance.

Afterward, most races have awards ceremonies—usually not as promptly as the officials may promise—accompanied by merchandise drawings, where there may be dozens of enticing prizes. If the weather's good, it's a great opportunity to sit on a sunny lawn, making new running friends as you ooh and ah at the speedy times turned in by the age-group winners— already planning your next race.

INDEX